Spiritual Gifts

Spiritual Gifts

For Today?
For Me?

John A. Lombard Jr.
Jerald J. Daffe

Pathway

Editor in Chief: James E. Cossey
Editor: Tom George
Editorial Assistant: Tammy Hatfield
Copy Editor: Jessica Tressler

Library of Congress Catalog Card Number: 2008930036
ISBN: 978-1-59684-306-6
Copyright © 2008 Pathway Press
Cleveland, Tennessee 37311

DEDICATED

to our wives,

Diana Meredith Lombard

and

Phyllis Della Lewis Daffe,

faithful companions

and

partners in ministry.

CONTENTS

ACKNOWLEDGMENTS

Appreciation to

Diana Meredith Lombard

and

Andrea Tormaschy

for keyboarding our manuscript.

FOREWORD

Jerald Daffe and John Lombard have teamed up to create a biblically sound, practical guide to spiritual gifts in the Church's ministry. Their perspective is clearly Pentecostal. They recognize the proliferation of spiritual gifts in many congregations today and address the need for pastoral guidance. Both coauthors are veterans of the Pentecostal Movement and have experiential knowledge of spiritual gifts. Both men share a ministry context that is pastoral and educational. They are engaged daily with men and women seeking to discover their own spiritual giftedness. They serve in a church community that looks to them for pastoral leadership on spiritual gifts. It is the years of pastoral experience and engagement in theological education that uniquely qualifies them to write on the subject of spiritual gifts.

Daffe and Lombard begin with an elemental question: "What is a spiritual gift?" They give counsel on how to discern or discover your spiritual gift. They explore the demonstration of spiritual gifts in the lives of select biblical characters. Then, they focus on the primary New Testament texts related to spiritual gifts: Ephesians 4, 1 Corinthians 12, and Romans 12. If you have wondered whether apostles and prophets should be a part of today's church ministry, they have a well-reasoned answer. If you want to know more about the charismatic gifts of prophecy, speaking in tongues, spiritual discernment, healing, wisdom, and so on, they provide a biblical perspective. If you want to better understand God's gifts for the Church's ministry, this book will help you.

A strength of the book and a reflection of the maturity of the coauthors is the final two chapters of the book. Chapter 12 addresses many misconceptions about spiritual gifts. Chapter 13 concludes the book with an exhortation to all Christians to use spiritual gifts in a loving manner that preserves the unity of the body of Christ. Daffe and Lombard know that spiritual gifts can be abused. Therefore, they emphasize that love is the true measure of spiritual maturity.

The message of this book speaks to an important need in today's church. The Charismatic Movement that began in the 1960s raised our awareness of spiritual gifts. The movement revitalized many churches in North America. Even so, it also plagued many churches through the undisciplined use of spiritual gifts. Pastors today are often perplexed about the demonstration of spiritual gifts in their congregations. They believe in the work of the Spirit among believers but they have reservations about the outcome of such activity. They know full well that the combination of human egos and spiritual gifts can be unpredictable. Moreover, many Christians seek a more significant relationship with God through the Spirit but do not understand the path to spiritual empowerment. This book will help both pastors and laypersons to know more fully the work of the Spirit through spiritual gifts.

The message of this book also speaks to key issues within the Charismatic/Pentecostal movement. Many churches within this faith tradition subscribe to the fivefold ministry of the church described in Ephesians 4. However, there is real disagreement about the role and identity of apostles and prophets in the contemporary church. There is also controversy about the practice of "impartation" of spiritual gifts and callings. This book addresses these issues and offers insights from a biblical perspective. Even if you disagree with the authors, you will find yourself challenged by their careful interpretation of Scripture.

Daffe and Lombard have served the body of Christ well in their collective wisdom on spiritual gifts presented in this book. The issue of spiritual gifts is critically important to fulfilling the mission of the Church. What better reason to read it?

—R. Jerome Boone, D.Min.
Academic Chair
Department of Christian Ministries
Lee University

INTRODUCTION

Whater does the average church need to make its ministry more effective?

More than likely if one were to poll a number of pastors, church members, and denominational leaders, we would discover some common, expected responses: dedicated members who support the mission and activities of the local congregation, expanded facilities to offer new programs, individuals who are gifted leaders on both the congregational and denominational levels, and more money to fund evangelism and benevolence. Each one of these definitely is legitimate.

The listed responses surely would include revival. Historically spiritual renewal must be an ongoing event in local churches and the greater denomination. The issue we then must face is how do we define the general term which is used so frequently? Surely all would agree it begins within the believers and then moves outside the four walls. Far too often revival is interpreted in terms of a series of meetings or some dramatic events. Easily overlooked is the spiritual development of believers in terms of recognizing and operating in one's spiritual giftedness.

Spiritual gifts are not limited to a few select individuals. The Holy Spirit intends for each believer to operate within a divinely imputed ability. Some are very public while others are just as important but behind the scenes. When believers discover their spiritual gifts and begin to operate within them, local churches will be edified. It brings a maturity that enables the Church to fulfill its biblical purpose.

It is our desire for believers to become knowledgeable about spiritual gifts and realize their potential for the Kingdom. We want to shout and sing, "Congratulations, you are gifted!"

Knowing our gifts in itself isn't sufficient. It then becomes our responsibility to allow the Holy Spirit to use us regardless of the time, place, or situation.

Congratulations, You're Gifted!

Edward L. Williams,
Irma M. B. & Marcy Williams

Irma B. Williams

Con - grat - u - la - tions, you're gift-ed!

Use your tal - ent for the glo - ry of the Lord;

— Your gifts are giv - en by the Fa-ther,_____ What-

ev - er you do, let His Name be a - dored;_____

Use your tal - ent for the glo - ry of the Lord, What-

Congratulations, You're Gifted!

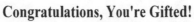

ev - er you do, let His Name be a - dored;____

_ Con - grat - u - la - tions, you're gift-ed!____

Use your tal - ent for the glo - ry of the Lord;

1

A Century
in Review

It seemed rather unusual that Sunday in the
late 1970s. The lone visitor in our evening service came early and sat on the front pew. During
the prayer request opportunity a visiting pastor
asked us to pray for the right person to come
to her church and lead revival services. Immediately our guest stood, turned to the visiting
pastor, and spoke.

"Sister, I'm a traveling apostle. I may be the
answer to your prayer."

Silent shock waves bounced throughout the congregation. Questions quickly arose. "Who is this
man?" "Who does he think he is?" "An apostle?"

This rarity of the past isn't true in the twenty-
first century. A review of selected Christian periodicals and books indicates a growing number
of individuals using the title and description of
apostle, prophet, and prophetess. Tied closely
to them are the terms *restoration* and *impartation*.

Since these aspects have not been a part of Classic Pentecostalism, some basic questions arise.

Do the spiritual gifts or spiritual offices of apostle and prophet exist today?

What have been and are the factors which foster this new emphasis?

How should we begin to evaluate these concepts?

Are spiritual gifts really that important to the Church?

Some may suggest no evaluation is necessary. "Let's just accept what comes as a new move of the Spirit for this time!" But blind acceptance isn't synonymous with faith. Genuine spirituality doesn't require us to put our intellect in a box, lock it, and throw away the key. We have an obligation to "try the spirits" and to be knowledgeable of both Scripture and Church history.

Some dangers exist if we adopt the non-evaluation perspective. First, it keeps individuals from developing spiritually, emotionally, and intellectually. They live in a state of not knowing for sure what truth is. Second, it opens the door for bondage at its worst, or a narrow perspective at its best. We have an obligation to God and to ourselves to know why we believe and why we practice certain actions.

Closely associated, and equally disastrous, is basic ignorance. Too many individuals are content to simply coast along, knowing they are believers and following those whom they like. A sense of blissful ignorance surrounds them. As a result, there's no development into mature, ministering Christians. Others seem to be in church settings that do not disciple them in the area of spiritual gifts. As a result, frequent misconceptions occur.

A classic example of the former was a young man's response on a spiritual gifts questionnaire. When asked to list his spiritual gift the response was "my smile." Later after a holistic, biblical study on spiritual gifts, he alternated between cringing and laughing at his previous answer.

Another young man listed his spiritual gift as "singing." Then he added, "I sure hope it is, because I like to sing and I am in a choir."

The answers of these young men raise a thought-provoking question. How many other Christians are in the same or similar state of mind?

Each of these examples/situations brings us to a major principle. What we believe needs to be the result of a heart and mind experience in accord with Scripture! Far too frequently we hear people say, "Well, that's just what I think." Not to be overlooked is the need for believers to know their spiritual gift and then minister through it! We need to be aware of God's equipping us for His service. Ministry to the church body isn't to be limited to a select few labeled as clergy.

With these concepts in mind, a brief historical review will provide a foundation for a discussion of spiritual gifts. In view of the scope of this book, the historical review will begin with early Pentecostalism of the twentieth century and continue into the current century.

EARLY PENTECOSTALISM

A common error of many people is to superimpose the present culture on the past and then proceed with unfair evaluations or accusations. This can easily occur when considering spiritual gifts. The greater emphasis on spiritual gifts in the latter twentieth century and initial decade of the twenty-first century cannot be found in the earlier years of the Pentecostal Movement. The early Pentecostals were not oblivious to spiritual gifts; however, it was not their primary focus.

Let's revisit the circumstances of those earlier decades. As "Holy Ghost" baptism swept through the United States and other countries, fledgling Pentecostal denominations came into existence. Some arose from a background of established Holiness groups while others sprang up anew. They were a direct result of the Azusa Street Revival. A common denominator was their doctrine of tongues as the initial evidence of the baptism of the Holy Spirit.

Where did they go from there? Unlike today, they had no Pentecostal theology books or periodicals to guide a further understanding of the fullness of the Holy Spirit's work. This would come only through continued study of the Scriptures and further experiencing the dimensions of the Holy Spirit's work in people's lives.

A concern/emphasis on spiritual gifts can be seen in three articles written in 1914 by A. J. Tomlinson, general overseer of the Church of God. The initial article titled "Pray! Pray! Pray!" offered insights on the perceived number of gifts and their evidence in the body.

> We have been patiently waiting for these gifts partially content with the slight manifestation we have realized but it is time now surely to meet conditions, get down in humility and pray and weep until these nine gifts are fully demonstrated and in use for God's glory and the salvation of many more of the human race will be saved.[1]

The next month Tomlinson wrote an impassioned plea for the evidence of the nine spiritual gifts:

> These gifts are manifested slightly at different times at different places, but let us press our claim on them until they will be manifested in their fullness and thus save from wreck and ruin many souls that will otherwise go down amid the storms of temptation poured in among them from the ranks for Satan and his host of blasphemous supporters.[2]

Three months later Tomlinson addressed the topic of spiritual gifts for a third time. As in the previous article, he emphasized the dangers that dominate the body unless spiritual gifts are operative.

> . . . so before the church will be the perfect body of our Lord she must have all these nine gifts in perfect operation. Without this equipment we are meeting with defeats and shipwrecks. Divisions, fanaticism, false teachings ruin and wrecked lives of many who once had a good experience are lying in heaps by the road sides.[3]

This early emphasis on the nine special gifts listed in 1 Corinthians 12:8-10 appeared to continue. However, the gifts of tongues, interpretation, and healing seemed to receive the greatest emphasis despite of the importance of all nine. There's no doubt tongues was the distinctive within Pentecostalism.

Later decades reflected this continued emphasis of the nine gifts. However, consideration was also given to the administration or ministry gifts of Ephesians 4:11. This can be seen in a 1949 *Evangel* article written by J. G. Hall.

> The gifts of the spiritual are nine in number and are clearly defined in 1 Corinthians 12:8-10. The second manifestation of the Spirit is called administration or ministries, and are five in number, as clearly desired in Ephesians 4:8-11.[4]

It appears safe to say the average Pentecostal believer heard of spiritual gifts but in reality was ill-informed concerning their breadth, their definition, and their operation. Emphasis on receiving the baptism of the Holy Spirit and sharing the full Gospel definitely took precedence. Several of the spiritual gifts were emphasized, but this whole dimension seemed to receive lower priority in doctrine and practice.

HEALING REVIVAL

The healing revival (1947-1958) deserves some consideration in any historical review of spiritual gifts. First, it brought a heightened emphasis on the gift of healing. Second, this dramatic move of the Holy Spirit would be a stimulus in the rise of the Charismatic Movement.

Divine healing as a doctrinal belief and practice definitely wasn't new to this time period since the more radical Holiness groups of the latter 1880s included healing as one of their distinctives. John Alexander Dowie, a Scottish-born Congregational preacher from Australia, brought healing to the foreground in the United States. In 1890 he formed the International Divine Healing Association, which was dedicated to spreading the message of divine healing.[5]

Dowie's ministry also included a vision of a special utopian-type city.

He had a vision of building an industrial city
without any institutional links with sin, disease and poverty. In Zion, Ill., there should be
neither liquor stores, theaters, pork abattoirs,
doctors nor hospitals; the latter were in any
case unnecessary in the holy city.[6]

God raised up two highly different individuals to initiate this new spiritual emphasis on
healing and the ministry of the Holy Spirit. They
were William Branham and Oral Roberts.

Though the Lord spoke to Branham at the age
of seven indicating he had a work for the boy to
do, he didn't become a believer until his early
twenties. He began as an ordained independent
Baptist minister who eventually was introduced
to the fullness of the Spirit by "oneness" people.
On May 7, 1946, he experienced an angelic visit
and was told he would be able to detect diseases
by vibrations in his hand. It always took place in
his left hand, enabling him to accurately discern
the particular disease. It is said he never mis-
diagnosed anyone in his healing line. Through
Branham's ministry came an emphasis not only
on healing but also the gift of knowledge. Not to
be overlooked is some people's believing Branham
had a prophetic identity with the task of being the
forerunner ushering in the Second Coming.[7]

Unlike the timid, simplistic Branham, Oral
Roberts quickly became a dynamic innova-
tor who would greatly impact the Charismatic

Movement and Pentecostalism. Miraculously healed of tuberculosis and stuttering, this son of a poor Pentecostal Holiness preacher accepted the call into ministry. In 1947 he resigned the last of four pastorates and launched an independent ministry headquartered in Tulsa. The healing of a polio victim able to now walk without braces quickly caused the healing emphasis to become dominant in his crusades.

Though Roberts was initially known for his healing ministry, he was a strong factor in laying the foundations for the Charismatic Movement. First, many people were introduced to the miraculous work of the Holy Spirit through his interdenominational meetings and the televised services. Second, his association with and encouragement of Demos Shakarian to bring into existence the vision for the Full Gospel Business Men's Fellowship International (FGBMFI) furthered the growth of the Charismatic Renewal.

LATTER RAIN MOVEMENT

The latter 1940s and early 1950s was the scene of some dynamic moves of the Holy Spirit. As previously mentioned, there was the rise of healing evangelists who would impact not only the United States and Canada but other countries as well. At the same time a number of colleges experienced dramatic spiritual renewals.

Scattered across the country colleges of various denominational affiliation saw extended services that shut down the class schedule as the chapel became the focus of the campus for days at a time. Lee College (now Lee University), Wheaton College, Asbury College, and Multnomah School of the Bible are a few of the schools so impacted in 1949 and 1950. It was in such a setting that we see the rise of what would become known as the Latter Rain Movement.

What would be labeled by opponents as the "New Order of the Latter Rain" found its beginnings in a revival at Sharon Bible School in North Battleford, Saskatchewan, Canada. The Sharon Orphanage and schools were established in 1947 by Reverend Herrick Holt of the local Church of the Four Square Gospel. The Bible school opened in October 1947, and by the following month twenty-five students received the baptism of the Holy Spirit.[8]

Holt was joined at North Battleford by George Hawtin, a former Pentecostal Assemblies minister; Erin Hawtin, a younger brother; and P. G. Hunt. These brethren, along with others, visited a William Branham crusade in Vancouver, British Columbia, in the fall of 1947. They were deeply impressed and influenced by Branham's gift of healing and the gift of knowledge of the illnesses prior to praying for people.

A second impacting force was the writings of healing evangelist Franklin Hall. He would write at least eighteen books; however, the most impacting and often mentioned one is *Atomic Power with God Through Prayer and Fasting*.

Believing the current Pentecostal Movement to be spiritually dry, Holt and his group returned to North Battleford and sought for a move of the Holy Spirit that would restore the gifts of the Spirit. School leaders and students alike engaged in fasting over a period of months. Some fasted for extended periods of time ranging from three to forty-two days. God rewarded their diligent seeking for revival. February 11-13, 1948, are the days that the spiritual restoration began. A prophecy was given of the revival that was about to take place. The next day, the 12th, a prophecy was given of God's desire to restore the gifts of the Spirit to those willing to receive them. Individuals were prayed for, healings took place, and some people began to manifest various gifts of the Spirit.

When word of this spiritual renewal spread abroad, people who were thirsting for the operation of the gifts came to North Battleford by the thousands. This revival movement spread to various cities, and the North Battleford brethren traveled to other places in the United States and Canada sharing both their experience and doctrine.

The distinctive beliefs, as well as some of the fringe ideas, were what would alienate this movement and eventually lead to its demise. However, we will quickly recognize some have resurfaced forty-five years later. Before looking at them specifically, it would be good to review their use of the term *latter rain*.

> It should be distinguished from early twenti-eth century Pentecostalism, which also used the idea of a "latter rain" as a central motif. The concept of the "latter rain" was thought by adherents to be rooted in the natural phenom-enon of Palestine of an early and latter rain.[10]

The latter or late rain was needed to bring the crop to maturity for harvesting (See Deut. 11:14; Joel 2:23; and Zech. 10:1). But from a spiritual perspective the outpouring of the Holy Spirit in Acts was the "early rain" and the last days manifestation of the Spirit the "latter rain."

Prophecy became a major distinctive of this movement. They saw the gift of prophecy as being foretold in Scripture as a sign of the last days. Included in this was the emphasis on per-sonal prophecies given by individual prophets or the prophetic presbytery. Some cautions were shared concerning the use of prophecy. It wasn't to be a guide for "people in every-day life, such as business, marriage or home life."[11]

Of great concern to Pentecostal denominations was the belief in present-day apostles and
prophets. Also causing controversy was the idea
of being able to impart spiritual gifts through
the laying on of hands. Included in this impartation was that of receiving the baptism of the
Holy Spirit in contrast to the normal practice of
"tarrying" to receive this blessing.

What could have been a major spiritual renewal became decimated with excesses and
false doctrines in less than two years. Following
is a short list of the difficulties.

1. An antidenominationalism referred to as
"undenominational" was fostered by emphasizing the authority of the elite spiritual leaders. Organization wasn't needed. People were
to follow the leading of the Spirit, especially as
presented by the traveling presbytery. Instead
of emphasizing the authority and ministry of elders in each location, the elders from North Battleford became the voice for all and thus known
as the "traveling presbytery."[12]

2. With prophecy being such a dominant distinctive it became the "in" thing, with people
manufacturing their own prophetic words and
conjectures.[13]

3. The concept of the manifestation of the sons
of God led to the doctrine of the "elect" receiving "redemptive bodies" here and now: ". . . any

person who died had not been able to 'appropriate the redemptive body' and was therefore not one of the 'overcomers.'"[14] In essence this view held to believers becoming divine here on earth.

4. There were other doctrines at odds with historical orthodoxy, "such as a denial of blood atonement, a denial of eternal hell, a belief in the ultimate deification of the church, and a belief in the ultimate reconciliation of the devil (although not everyone in this movement believed all of these doctrines)."[15]

In 1949 the Assemblies of God General Council meeting in Seattle adopted a resolution disapproving the practices of this "New Order of the Latter Rain." Specifically listed were the beliefs of the Church being built on the foundation of present-day apostles and prophets and the confessing to and deliverance from sin by humans. Also included were the practices of imparting gifts by the laying on of hands and the misuses of prophetic utterances.[16]

Many years later George Hawtin reflected rather sadly about some of their beliefs and practices.

> There was to be no fellowship with anybody what was not within the confines of our ever narrowing circle. We were the elect. We stood on the foundation and all other men stood on sinking stand. No man must cast out a devil

unless he followed us. . . . We were the most spiritual people in the world. We were going to reign
in the Kingdom and even now we were beginning
to reign. We had the gifts of the Spirit and we were
going to "call the shots" in the Tribulation.[17]

(A personal note: As a boy I remember my dad
dealing with the negative impact of the latter
rain doctrines. As a district overseer he met with
a congregation being split over this new super-
spirituality. When about to take a new pastorate,
he received a phone call from the members saying, "Don't come. We don't need a pastor. We just
follow the Spirit's leading." Within a relatively
short time this church closed its doors.)

THE CHARISMATIC RENEWAL

The rise of the Charismatic Renewal fostered
some important questions among Pentecostals.
They are:

1. How can Protestants and Catholics receive
the baptism of the Holy Spirit outside of a Pentecostal setting (church or home)?

2. How can a Holy Spirit baptized believer continue to attend a mainline Protestant
church?

3. How can anyone claim to be a Spirit-filled
believer and not follow the traditional guidelines of holiness?

Of greater discussion and dissension would

be the issue of Spirit baptism and the gifts of the Spirit. Within the renewal movement there would be no umbrella acceptance of tongues as the initial evidence of Spirit baptism. There also would be an emphasis on the operation of all the gifts of the Spirit and their being one of many possible evidences of Spirit baptism.

The formative years of this renewal were in the 1940s and 1950s when many mainline Protestants experienced Spirit baptism. However, news of this came very slowly to Pentecostals. The emergence of this spiritual renewal into a major impacting movement occurred between 1958 and 1974.

The Charismatic Movement definitely brought a renewed emphasis to the role of spiritual gifts. Possibly the greatest contribution in this area was the emphasis on the broad range of gifts instead of the narrow consideration of only a few such as so frequently seen within Pentecostalism. A few people went so far as to suggest Pentecostals were cultic or bordering on heresy for having such a narrow practical perspective. No doubt this was an overstatement, but it does bear some consideration.

Some of the seeds of the Latter Rain Movement took root and grew within the Charismatic Renewal. One such emphasis was on the gift of prophecy. Another would be the growing practice of laying on hands to receive specific experiences or gifting.

An example of this was Kenneth Hagin's statement: "The gift of faith operates though me and I impart the Holy Ghost to people by laying on of hands."[18] This concept of impartation would definitely be popularized in the following decades.

Not to be forgotten or overlooked is the Vineyard church network. Founded by John Wimber from a congregation in Yorba Linda, California, this network of churches provided a nonthreatening means of Charismatic expression to many Protestants. Spiritual gifts, including the prophetic, became a definite aspect of their ministry. For a period of time both the Kansas City Fellowship and the congregation known for the "Toronto Blessing" were a part of the extended Vineyard family of churches. From Wimber's beginning pastorate in 1978 until his death on November 17, 1997, this network grew to almost five hundred churches.[19]

THE PROPHETIC AND APOSTOLIC RENEWAL MOVEMENTS

The last decades of the twentieth century were the scene of two distinct movements that had roots in the Latter Rain. In the 1980s it was the rise of an emphasis on the office of prophet and the role of prophecy in the individual lives of believers and the corporate life of congregations. Immediately following, in the 1990s, came the apostolic emphasis on the office of apostle with varying concepts of their ministry and authority. Together these emphases placed special attention on Ephesians 4:11 and the fivefold ministry.

Since the chapter on prophets and apostles will share the broader aspects of these movements, we simply bring attention to them here as part of the twentieth century review on the role of spiritual gifts.

ENDNOTES

[1] A. J. Tomlinson, "Pray! Pray! Pray," *The Church of God Evangel* 24 Jan. 1914: 1.

[2] A. J. Tomlinson, "Pray! Pray! Pray," *The Church of God Evangel* 21 Feb. 1914: 4.

[3] A. J. Tomlinson, "More About the Gifts," *The Church of God Evangel* 16 May 1914: 2.

[4] J. G. Hall, "Gifts, Administrations and Operations," *The Church of God Evangel* 1 Oct. 1949: 4.

[5] C. Douglas Weaver, *The Healer-Prophet, William Marrion Branham* (Macon: Mercer University Press, 1987) 42.

[6] Walter J. Hollenwager, *The Pentecostals* (Minneapolis: Augsburg Publishing House, 1972) 117.

[7] Weaver, 27-28.

[8] Richard M. Riss, *Latter Rain* (Missassauga: Honeycomb Visual Productions, LTD, 1987) 60.

[9] Riss, 60-61

[10] Robin M. Johnston, "Latter Rain" in *Encyclopedia of Pentecostal and Charismatic Christianity*, ed. Stanley M. Burgess (New York: Routledge, 2006) 285.

[11] These guidelines are found in the November 1948 issue of the *Sharon Star*. Riss, *Latter Rain*, 81.

[12] Riss, 63-64.

[13] David Pytches, *Some Said It Thundered*, (Nashville: Oliver Nelson, 1991) 12.

[14] Riss, 96.

[15] Burgess, *Encyclopedia of Pentecostal and Charismatic Christianity*, 166.

[16] Riss, 119.

[17] Riss, 97.

[18] Kenneth Hagin, *The Holy Spirit and His Gifts* (Tulsa: Rhema Bible Church, 1974) 89.

[19] Joe Maxwell, "Vineyard Founder Wimber Dies," *Christianity Today* Jan. 12, 1988: 58.

STUDY GUIDE
Chapter 1

The current emphasis on spiritual gifts can be traced to varied movements during the twentieth century. In tracing them we are reminded of two important truths. First, God uses a variety of individuals to bring the truths of Scripture known and operating within the body of Christ. Second, the blessings of spiritual gifts are not to be taken lightly or loosely since such attitudes can open the door to destructive heresies.

At this point in your life, how much have you studied or been exposed to biblical preaching and teaching on spiritual gifts? More than likely, you cannot put a numerical evaluation on the specific times and places. But, most of us can suggest responses such as little, some, considerable, or a great deal. Regardless of where you fit on this scale, it is hoped you will have grown in information through this historical review.

QUESTIONS

1. What are several concepts shared by A. J. Tomlinson in his three 1914 articles?

2. How different were Branham and Roberts, though both laid foundations for events of the 1980s and 1990s?

3. How did the Latter Rain Movement set the stage for the Prophetic Movement of later decades?

4. What were some of the doctrines and practices which discredited the Latter Rain?

5. How did the Charismatic Movement impact the role of spiritual gifts?

6. Which scriptural passage became an emphasis verse in the 1980s and 1990s?

2

The Sources of Our Giftedness

Congratulations, you're gifted!
Use your talent for the glory of the Lord;
Your gifts are given by the Father,
Whatever you do, let His name be adored;

Use your talent for the glory of the Lord,
Whatever you do, let His name be adored;
Congratulations, you're gifted!
Use your talent for the glory of the Lord.
                                        Lyrics by Irma B. Williams

Just as the words of the song say, we echo, "Congratulations, you're gifted!" Yes, every one of us is a gifted person. Occasionally, there are individuals with low self-images who believe they "can't really do anything." Everyone else is seen as talented and able to do so much more.

Sadly, these people perceive having more or being "up-front" as the scale to judge one's talents or gifts. This may lead to their withdrawing from serving or being reluctant to do what is within their personal ability.

On the opposite side are those individuals who appear to be God's gift here on earth. They can do so many things well. These "Renaissance people" seem to excel in a broad cross section of areas. One wonders if there is anything they can't do. Of course, there is! We just aren't in the position to see their failures or avoidances.

Could it be we may have a faulty concept of what it means to be gifted when it comes to our spiritual lives? School systems have programs for the "gifted and talented" students whose academic attributes are above their peers. This advanced placement provides opportunities that are consistent with their abilities. They are not better people. It's matter of skill level and diligence. The same is true for each of us. As will be more specifically addressed in a later chapter, the apostle Paul in 1 Corinthians 12 emphasized the value of each person and their giftedness. Each plays a vital part in the local body of Christ just as each of our body parts contributes to the function of the whole. An abscessed tooth or badly bruised toe quickly reminds us of their impact on the whole person. In the same way, when a believer chooses not to be used of the Spirit in their giftedness, the body of Christ suffers. This should be an encouragement for each of us to become sensitive to our areas of giftedness and open to opportunities for ministry.

ORIGIN OF ALL GIFTS

When you hear or think of the word *gifts*, what images come to mind? Where do your thoughts immediately focus?

Wrapped packages?

A money gift card?

A certain vehicle?

Maybe a trip?

Possibly friendship appears?

Regardless which of the preceding suggestions or others that may be offered, they all have one thing in common. Each is not self-generated. They do not appear because of personal skill, value, or purchase. Each one stems from a source other than itself.

To be gifted in any area of life automatically assumes a giver. Someone other than ourselves makes it possible for each of us to have a wide array of physical and spiritual abilities. As believers, we know this doesn't originate in chance happenings of a supposed evolutionary process. The Bible clearly presents God as the source for all things that exist, except sin.

A review of the initial chapters of the Book of
Genesis quickly reminds us of God's being the
originator of all gifts that we enjoy. Consideration also needs to be given to how our limitations may be seen as a form of giftedness, as will
be seen in Adam. It allows for diversity. We all
aren't the same. How boring it would be if we
were! It emphasizes the need for each other in
order to live as a family and greater community.
Limitations, hopefully, allow us more time to
develop the talents/gifts that we have.

God created Adam to be unfulfilled though
surrounded by the beauty of the earth and the
companionship of animals. There was the need
of someone of like nature to fill the void. Only
through the union of the two separate genders
were there completion and the means for con-
tinuation of the human race. Within this couple
was the possibility for difference within their
children, not only as it relates to gender but also
for personality, preferences, and abilities.

The first two named children of Adam and
Eve reflected their inherent differences. Cain
worked as a farmer while Abel, was a shepherd (Gen. 4:2). The elder brother demonstrated a desire to do worship his way while
the younger followed God's plan. In anger at
both God and Abel, Cain chose the violence of
murder.

Continuing in the genealogy of Cain there was the appearance of some positive gifts or talents originating with specific descendants. Musical abilities (the arts) arose with Jubal (v. 21). Then there was Tubal-Cain, who became skilled using different metals to forge or hammer out many kinds of tools (v. 22). Notice how one's skills provided enjoyment and entertainment and the other's ability was very practical and an aid to daily work.

We must also consider the other dimension of our giftedness—the spiritual. John 4:24 reminds us of God's being spirit. We must know the source of spiritual gifts. Nothing spiritual can arise out of the material. This will be covered in greater detail in other sections, but it is vital to see God as the originator of all gifts.

ORIGIN OF NATURAL GIFTS

God wants to work through our lives. He seeks the best for us and our service to His kingdom. This doesn't mean we are put together like robots with the master engineer determining every capability. Who we are in terms of our abilities is not necessarily divinely orchestrated. It seems safe to say the vast majority of our talents and giftedness stem from natural or human circumstances. Consider the following four:

First is a person's gene pool. Maybe you have heard someone say, "It's in the genes, man, it's in the genes," to explain either their ability or inability. A recent cartoon showed a little boy trying to express this same concept. Only it came out, "It's in the pants, in the pants." He definitely was thinking of the word *jeans*. Genetic inheritance determines a great number of things such as height, body build, facial appearance, and hair color, as well as certain peculiarities. Just recently, a person was heard to say, "I have flat feet just like my dad." If you have a child who is left-handed, the common question offered is, "Do you have anyone else in your family who is left-handed?" The answer: "Oh yes, my wife's father, her twin brother, and an older sister."

Maybe you have seen a couple who neither stand close to 5'10". Their son is a towering 6'7". Two questions immediately surface: Is he adopted? Or, does he have a growth hormone problem? The real answer is grandparents and great-uncles of considerable height. Yes, it skipped a generation but still is part of the gene pool.

Many other abilities may be transmitted through our parentage. Musical skills (vocal or instrumental), analytical abilities, and artistic creativity are other gifts that may be contained within our genetic heritage. At times, we may be painfully aware of the seemingly unfair distribution of our gene pool. One sibling inherits a natural ability, but another is left out of that particular skill.

A second contributing factor to our natural gifts is the environment in which we were raised or lived for a considerable period of time. Either out of necessity or common involvement, skills and principles are learned and become embedded in who we are. Parents and grandparents, as well as neighbors and friends, may enable us to be skilled in tasks such as mechanics, cooking, gardening, and construction, to name a few. People skills and communication skills may also be gained. Not to be forgotten is learning to be a compassionate, caring person willing to go out of your way to be of help.

Several years ago, while sitting in a circle of college students discussing the results of their having taken a spiritual gifts test, one of the young men stated it appeared he had the gift of hospitality. Since follow-up was a part of this group experience, and knowing he was single and had never had an apartment, I asked a leading question.

"Did your mom and dad have people regularly stay in their home?"

"Yes, they did," he answered.

A second question followed: "Could it be you think of being hospitable because of being raised to do so rather than being spiritually gifted?"

After some reflection, he agreed it very likely was true. This setting was so different from what two young men presented in another discussion. They informed the group of their practice of looking for a homeless traveler and offering him a place to stay overnight in their apartment. Upon hearing of their hospitality, everything within me was screaming, "How stupid can you get? Don't you know of all the perverts and mentally ill who are wandering the streets and roads of our country!" But then I was checked in my spirit. Isn't that truly hospitality? Though offering cautions to them, who was I to even suggest a true gifting be discarded because of its unusual nature.

A third factor contributing to natural gifting is experience. At times, this may appear to be closely tied to environment. But, for our discussion let's separate it and see it in terms of events over a more extended period of time. Another way to look at it is "life experience." Generally, living brings "hard knocks" and "opportunities" to all of us. We are placed in situations that stretch us and provide knowledge as well as wisdom for the future. Through these, we attain some forms of natural gifting.

As a result of experience, we are able to say and to do what will be of the greatest help to another person in their need. In some cases, the person may think you are the divine messenger of the Lord. But you know the truth. It wells up from the depth of experience and relationship with Him. By the way, growing older does have some great advantages. One's expanding experiences should enable us to be greater sources of knowledge and wisdom.

The desperation in the young man's voice was evident over the telephone. "I have to talk to you . . . tonight!"

"But I'm not free until ten thirty this evening. What about tomorrow morning?"

"I can't wait," he replied. "Ten thirty is just fine. I'll come to your office"

Later that evening he poured out his fears of some physical symptoms and the stress of his overload. Though deeply concerned about him, inside I was smiling and saying, "Been there, done that." My counsel, which he gratefully accepted, wasn't from a spiritual giftedness. It came from being in that same situation less than ten years before. I understood his fears and struggles. But I also knew how they could be overcome.

The fourth factor impacting our natural gifting is education. Regardless of the discipline area, education greatly expands one's knowledge base. This in turn increases a person's overall comprehension of other areas as well. Education also impacts one's practical abilities, some educational programs or opportunities more than others. If that were not to happen, education would surely be a waste of time and money! But the bottom line continues to be this: education is only a factor in developing or initiating a natural gift. It is not the means by which a spiritual gift develops in the believer's life.

ORIGIN OF SPIRITUAL GIFTS

To ensure a productive discussion on any topic it is important for each of the participants to have the same understanding or definition of the terms. For example, a Christmas greeting note wished us a "nano Christmas." The dictionary definition indicated a measurement of one billionth. Knowing this friend, surely he wasn't wishing us a small or dwarf celebration. In humor, a colleague suggested it sounded like a "hip grandmother." My student secretary stated it meant really good or great. The latter definitely sounded best!

Spiritual gifts are manifestations of the Holy Spirit in the lives of believers enabling them to minister in a means beyond their human capacity. Believers receive these gifts as a result of God's grace. They are not intended to bring personal glory. The purpose of each gift is for service within the church, the body of Christ in general and the local body of assembled believers.

Spiritual gifts are supernatural abilities given by God and manifested through the empowerment of the Holy Spirit. They are "God-given abilities demonstrated through believers by the Holy Spirit."[1]

The foundational verse for the origin of spiritual gifts is 1 Corinthians 12:4-6:

> There are different kinds of gifts, but the same Spirit. There are different kinds of service, but the same Lord. There are different kinds of working, but the same God works all of them in all men (NIV).

Immediately we are presented with the diversity of spiritual gifts. This can easily be seen as one progresses further in the chapter to the listings. There definitely is a tremendous difference between the gift of healing and the gift of administration. The same can be said for the gift of wisdom and the gift of interpretation. However, this diversity neither minimizes or maximizes some nor indicates a variety of origins.

These verses also emphasize spiritual gifts originating from the entire Godhead—Father, Son, and Holy Spirit. It's vitally important for us to see the totality of the Godhead in the operation of these gifts. Even though the gifts and their operation initially direct our attention to the Holy Spirit, we must see the coordinated role of the Father and the Son. They are not independent manifestations.

It becomes readily apparent these gifts are not further enhancements of one's natural abilities. There is no way possible for an individual to suddenly speak intelligently a foreign language in which they were not raised or formally instructed. Neither can a person through their natural ability initiate or complete healing of diseases or crippling conditions in another person. No matter how much a person may desire for someone to be raised from the dead, it never will be accomplished by simple human effort.

The parallel between some of the spiritual gifts and natural abilities is also evident. This, however, does not support the concept of some gifts just being enhancements of one's inherent ability. Teaching and administration are two dominant examples. Some individuals are excellent teachers. They present materials in an interesting, analytical, understandable manner. It stems from a variety of influences such as personality, adaptation of good teaching methods, understanding people's learning methods, and formal instructional education. Other individuals are superb administrators. They can organize, troubleshoot, handle personnel, and maintain progress with an eye for the future. Again, like natural teachers, these skilled administrators have natural organizational skills, have been mentored in leadership skills, have a passion for the task at hand, and often follow the patterns/methods of successful leaders.

Other individuals are excellent teachers and administrators as a result of being spiritually gifted. They are empowered though the action of the Holy Spirit to accomplish what is not evident in their lives through any natural means. Through God's grace their gifts become operable for the benefit of the church. Yes, once the gift is imprinted within one's life there is the need to learn how to better operate within it. But it doesn't change the source of its origination, God himself.

Remember the account of Simon recorded in Acts 8. For an extended period of time, he amazed people with his magic and they followed him. Then Philip came to Samaria. Simon followed him "everywhere, astonished by the great signs and miracles" (Acts 8:13 NIV). When Peter and John came as representatives of the apostles in Jerusalem, individuals received the baptism of the Holy Spirit. At that point Simon assumed the power to be of an origin that enabled it to be purchased. Instead of a deal, he received a stinging rebuke.

The bottom line for the origination of spiritual gifts is simply this: All spiritual gifts are divinely originated and imputed into believers for the edification of the body of Christ and its ministry.

RECOGNIZING YOUR GIFT

The sanctifying work of the Holy Spirit in salvation not only puts us in right relationship with our Heavenly Father but also opens the door to our spiritual gifting. Facing each believer is the challenge of recognizing their specific spiritual gift(s). Complicating this are three particular difficulties: no biblical formula for recognition, no specific timetable, and no initial signal/sign of its imputation. It's no wonder some believers struggle with the issue of identifying their spiritual giftedness. However, all is not lost or simply relative. Following are four helps:

A popular means is to take a spiritual gifts test. The various tests have some value. A tremendous caution flag needs to be inserted here. They are not absolute, infallible indicators. First, the test, no matter how good, cannot separate one's natural gifts from his/her spiritual gifts. Second, the test is based on a person's memory, perception, and interpretation of how many times make up an answer of "much" or "some." Third, the test's accuracy is based on a person's having a certain amount of experience.

The greetings page on the inner cover of the Wagner-Modified Houts Questionnaire contains an extremely important qualifier that seems to be regularly overlooked by both those administering it and those taking it. It reads as follows:

". . . do not regard the results of this test as final. The three or four gifts on which you score highest may or may not be your real spiritual gifts. Nevertheless, they are a starting point for prayer and experimentation. You will need other members of the body of Christ to help you confirm what gifts you have as well as what gifts you might not have. If you are under twenty five years of age or if you have been a Christian for fewer than six months, treat the results of this questionnaire a bit more tentatively than otherwise because the questions are based on actual past experience."

A second potential indicator of a spiritual gift is a growing passion and ability that previously did not exist. As the Holy Spirit begins to stir within and to provide a new compulsion, this may be the release of a spiritual gift. Why now rather than previously? Several answers readily come to mind. (1) There is a need for this gift within the body of people with whom you associate. (2) You are now spiritually mature enough for this gift's operation. (3) Another possibility is your being in a state of submission or openness for the Holy Spirit to work through you.

An example of this would be the retirement statement of a layman who for a number of years ran a bus ministry in the projects. A few of the sentences went something like this: "I was repulsed by dirty children with runny noses.

But God gave me such a love for them. I hold them and no longer am concerned about their physical appearance."

A new ability, not the result of education, practice, or copying, suddenly begins to arise within. This third setting should most definitely be a help or indicator. Initially, it may be frightening because of the tremendous responsibility which comes with it. A certain level of fear may also arise because of not initially feeling comfortable with this gift. But, in the middle of this apprehension should be the growing awareness of God's gifting.

A fourth help in identifying one's spiritual giftedness is the observation and encouragement of mature believers. Though experience and discernment these men and women often are able to detect the evidence of a gift even before the person becomes aware. Or, they are able to encourage and to fan the flames of what is being ignited. Here again, a caution needs to be inserted. No one should claim a particular gift simply because another believer suggests its presence. However, this encouragement may be a signal to explore the possibility.

ENDNOTES

[1] French Arrington, *Encountering the Holy Spirit* (Cleveland, TN: Pathway Press, 2003) 238.

[2] C. Peter Wagner, "Finding Your Spiritual Gifts," Gospel Light, 2005.

STUDY GUIDE
Chapter 2

This chapter reminded us how every gift indicates a giver. The challenge for each of us is to carefully evaluate our abilities to determine if it is a natural gift or a spiritual gift. An important factor to remember is that spiritual gifts are not the enhancement of our natural gifts. They are supernatural abilities given by God and manifested by the empowerment of the Holy Spirit.

Do you happen to see yourself as one of those individuals in the opposite positions of spiritual giftedness? If you do, work at moving to a place of reality in terms of God's gifting you in both the natural and the spiritual. Each of us can play a vital role in the function of the local church in particular and the body of Christ in general.

QUESTIONS

1. How does the Creation account in Genesis demonstrate God's being the originator of all gifts?

2. In what ways do Cain and Abel demonstrate inherent differences?

3. What is our "gene pool"?

4. How can environment impact one's giftedness?

5. What role does experience play in our abilities?

6. What are spiritual gifts?

7. Why are spiritual gifts not just enhancements of natural gifts?

8. List the four possible helps in determining one's spiritual gifts.

3

Spiritual Giftedness in the Old Testament

On the first day of lecture/discussion in an introductory Bible class, I asked my students, "How old is old?" Even though this was a Message of the Old Testament class, the students immediately associated the question with a person's chronological age. Usually the answers were offered with a great deal of caution.

A few of the bolder students suggested several numbers. Then one young lady raised her hand and asked, "How old are you?"

"Does it really matter?" was my response.

Across the classroom heads nodded in agreement. They didn't want to start the semester by offending the professor.

A second question was then offered.

"What are some synonyms or other associations you place with the word *old*?"

"Comfortable."

"Great-grandparents."

"Antique."

"Worn out."

"Outdated."

This representative list of their responses quickly indicated a sense of being more non-applicable. The same approach is often taken by believers toward the Old Testament. Yes, it is true Jesus came and provided a new covenant and we have a direct relationship to our Heavenly Father. Many of the old guidelines are no longer a part of the believer's life. However, to simply ignore or easily bypass the Old Testament is to neglect foundational principles that continue in the New Testament and today. One such area is the work of the Holy Spirit during the Old Testament era.

OLD TESTAMENT REVIEW

Though the intent of this chapter is to highlight evidences of spiritual giftedness in the Old Testament, it seems necessary to briefly review the work of the Holy Spirit in this era. In his classic work, *What the Bible Says About the Holy Spirit*,[1] Stanley Horton devoted three chapters to the work of the Holy Spirit in the Old Testament. His approach provides the framework for our abbreviated reminder of the Spirit's ministry in the previous millennia.

It is easy to fall into the trap of assuming the Holy Spirit's real work began on the day of Pentecost with the dramatic outpouring on those obediently waiting in Jerusalem. The phenomena described in Acts 2:1-4 provide a dynamic picture of this new dimension of the Spirit's work. No longer would there be just a few who experience His empowerment. Instead, it would become inclusive as prophesied by Joel (2:28-29). Peter immediately pointed the gathered crowd to understanding this to be the fulfillment of Joel's prophecy (Acts 2:16-18).

In the same way Peter wanted them to know of prophetic fulfillment, we need to understand the ongoing work of the Holy Spirit from the beginning of the biblical record. Maybe here is a good place for us to make sure we have a correct doctrinal stance as it relates to the Holy Spirit. First, the Holy Spirit is an equal member of the Trinity along with the Father and Son. He isn't a later creation by the Father and/or Son. He isn't a force that can be referred to as an "it." He isn't a silent partner who suddenly was inserted into the human drama.

At various times throughout the early centuries of the Christian church, individuals fostered heretical doctrines about the Spirit's origin and relationship within the Trinity. Each time, church councils met, condemned the heresy, and upheld a true theology that can be summarized with three dimensions of equality: the Holy Spirit is coeternal, co-substantial, and co-legal with the other members of the Trinity.

Because of the eternal plan we only see glimpses of the Holy Spirit's work in the Old Testament. However, each of them reveals to us His activity and empowering. From the beginning of time as related in the Book of Genesis, the Spirit was active. This involvement was then seen in the lives of specific individuals such as the patriarchs, Israel's leadership, the judges, and the prophets. These accounts provide us with a limited view of Spirit empowerment and giftedness that would later become widespread.

Before looking at the examples of giftedness, let's be reminded of the Spirit's involvement in Creation (Gen. 1). Even before the specific events of each of the Creation days, we see the Spirit's moving or hovering over the Earth. What was He doing? Why was He there? These are good questions for which no specific answer assuredly can be given. Of importance to us is His activeness prior to the distinct events that will follow.

After verse 2, we find a second reference to the Spirit's involvement. On day six of the Creation week, after having created the warm-blooded animals, God used the plural pronoun *us* as He prepared to create humankind. There was no one else for this to refer to other than the members of the Godhead. The Trinity—composed of Father, Son, and Holy Spirit—created humankind. Besides the plural pronoun *us* in verse 26, the plural adjective *our* was used several times. Since there is unity in the Trinity, the Holy Spirit was an active participant.

Following the Creation account the Old Testament records the work of the Holy Spirit in relationship to select individuals. It readily becomes apparent they were in roles of leadership of varying responsibility. The Spirit empowered and gifted them according to the need, based on position and purpose.

INDIVIDUAL GIFTEDNESS

The method of approach becomes the real challenge here. Do we list specific spiritual gifts and then insert individuals who qualify? Or, do we use select people and reflect on their being gifted by the Holy Spirit? Both have merit. However, the love for studying the individual lives of biblical characters becomes a major factor thus influencing the choice of the latter as the major means. Only the ministry gift/position of prophet will be considered as a separate entity.

MOSES

Moses' call to lead Israel out of Egyptian slavery was definitely a miraculous setting. Herding sheep out in the desert, he saw an unusual phenomenon—a bush that burned but wasn't consumed (Ex. 3:3). God spoke directly to Moses and offered miraculous signs by which to confirm to the people his commission (4:1-9). He would be used to perform mighty miracles; however, it isn't until much later in the narrative that there is a specific reference to the Holy Spirit's work in and through Moses' life.

Moses operated in the ministry gift of prophet. This was strongly revealed in Numbers 12:6-8 as God rebuked Miriam and Aaron for speaking against Moses. But he was no ordinary prophet in terms of how God revealed Himself and His will. There was a face-to-face relationship.

The reference to the Spirit's being on Moses (11:17) came in the middle of a major problem. Once again rebelliousness arose within the people. They were wailing at the entrances of their tents and bemoaning not having the foods of Egypt. Totally overlooked is their previous bondage. Frustrated, Moses shared the troubling questions of his inner being. In response God said He would take of the Spirit that was on Moses and put Him in the elders of Israel to share the load.

Moses did not impart the anointing and Spirit on these tribal leaders. God alone made the decision and accomplished the task. Those men evidenced the Spirit's coming upon them by prophesying. It did not, however, remain as a gift to be repeated at other times (v. 25).

Several other observations are included. First, note Moses' desire for all the people to have the Spirit dwelling on them and prophesying.

Second, though Moses served as the divinely ordained leader of Israel, there was no hint of his having the spiritual gift of leadership or administration. Otherwise, it is doubtful Moses' father-in-law would have had to show the error of his way and the need for delegation (Ex. 18).

Third, many miracles were performed through Moses. Maybe there is sufficient evidence to suggest the gift of miracles working in and through Moses. He was used to alter the normal causes or forces of nature such as the opening of the Red Sea, water from a rock, and sweetening bitter water.

SAMSON

Samson stands as the only judge whose life was shared from birth to death. We have no indication of his physical size, though pictorially he is usually portrayed as quite muscular. This might be accurate in that once captured by the Philistines he worked exceptionally hard labor at a grinder. If not careful, we can become guilty of too much emphasis on his ability and too little emphasis of the Holy Spirit's strengthening him to accomplish superhuman feats.

The question that faces us is whether the Holy Spirit dwelled within Samson or simply came upon him at select times. If the Spirit dwelled within, then we may assume the gift of miracles to be evident. However, if there was no gifting in miracles, we must believe in a man of highly unusual strength due to the many feats where there is no statement of the Spirit moving through Samson at that time.

While Samson was a young man, the Spirit began to stir within him. It would seem this was the point of Samson's experiencing the "moving" of the Holy Spirit in his life (Judg. 13:25). If it means the Spirit's coming upon and dwelling within, it appears acceptable to assume giftedness in miracles. When the Lord departed from Samson after he revealed the source of his strength to Delilah it also means the absence of the Holy Spirit (16:20). The Spirit would no longer be operable in his life.

ELISHA

Elisha's ministry spanned some sixty years as the leading citizen of Israel, the Northern Kingdom. He was the anointed successor to Elijah, God's most powerful prophet raised up to confront Israel's most wicked king, Ahab. These were big shoes to fill. No wonder his request was to receive a double portion of Elijah's spirit. He wasn't requesting to be twice as great. This must be understood within the framework of the eldest son's receiving a double portion of a father's inheritance.

Elisha's ministry gift or position was one of a prophet. His reputation as God's spokesperson was even known to Jehoshaphat, king of Judah. When Jehoshaphat asked for a prophet of the Lord and was told of Elisha's presence, he stated, "The word of the Lord is with him" (2 Kings 3:12). Within this position, the gift of miracles becomes evident. Sixteen separate miracles are recorded ranging from raising a boy from the dead to causing an ax head to float. No other prophet in the Bible ministered so often in the area of miracles.

The gift of knowledge can be seen on one occasion. After Naaman received healing by following the instructions to dip seven times in the Jordan, he returned to Elisha's home with the intent of sharing a gift of gratitude. Elisha's refusal was noted by his servant and perceived as letting Naaman "get off too easy." Fabricating a story of two young prophets just arriving and Elisha's desire for a set of clothing for each and some silver, he followed Naaman's party. Naaman graciously included a second talent of silver.

On his return, Elisha immediately confronted Gehazi and accurately recited what took place. Because of the Spirit's gifting of Elisha, Gehazi would have a legacy of leprosy because of succumbing to a greed for materialism.

BEZALEL AND OHOLIAB

The spiritual gifting of these two men differed greatly from that of any other biblical example. Neither of them held a ministry position such as prophet. Nor was either of them a selected political or military leader of Israel. Frequently these two men are described as artisans to whom the Lord gave special ability. There is no statement of their being skilled prior to the Lord's Spirit filling and gifting (read Ex. 35:30—36:2) However, in view of their gifting it seems logical they were.

To fully grasp the significance of this gifting, one must recognize the context in which it occurred. Israel was encamped at Mount Sinai. Here they would be organized both politically and religiously. While there, God gave Moses very specific details concerning the building of the Tabernacle, furnishings, and courtyard (chs. 25-27, 36-38). Not to be overlooked are the distinct descriptions for the priests' garments (chs. 28, 39). This nation was camped far from the centers of civilization and whatever specific tools and other resources for crafting would normally be available. In this primitive setting, God spiritually gifted two men to fulfill the monumental task of producing the product as well as teaching others to help in the project.

Two gifts are specifically mentioned here, wisdom and teaching. Wisdom enables one to take information/knowledge and apply it to the task at hand. They were facing a major project with specific details. Keep in mind Israel's stay at Mount Sinai was only thirteen months. Once all the materials were gathered, these two men would organize as well as teach others the "what" and "how" of the necessary tasks. Even the skilled artisans who came to accomplish the work would need guidance so that everything was exactly as God prescribed (35:10).

Through the giftedness of Bezalel and Oholiab, along with their workers, the Tabernacle was constructed. Notice how two references emphasize the work being completed "just as the Lord had commanded" (39:32, 43).

JOSEPH AND DANIEL

Though separated in time by approximately one thousand years, these two men had a great deal in common. Both lived a righteous life regardless of the potential consequences. Each experienced God's deliverance from difficult circumstances—prison and a lions' den. They were placed in positions of leadership within powerful kingdoms of the ancient world. And, each of them was used in the gift of interpretation.

Normally when thinking of interpretation we associate it within the framework of someone speaking in tongues and then an interpretation being given. Joseph and Daniel demonstrated a gifting in interpretation but in different settings. Both of them were used to interpret dreams.

Joseph's association with dreams began in the scriptural record with his personal dreams. In each case, his family recognized the inherent symbolism. He didn't offer an interpretation (Gen. 37:1-11). Many years later while a prisoner in Egypt, he interpreted two dreams for former employees of Pharaoh (ch. 40). When Joseph inquired of the reason for their sadness, each told him of having a dream but no one to interpret. Joseph immediately testified as to the ultimate source of interpretation and then shared the meaning of each man's dream.

Several years later when Pharaoh dreamed and no one could interpret, the cupbearer remembered Joseph. When Pharaoh indicated Joseph was a dream interpreter, he once again pointed to God as the interpreter. After hearing the dreams, Joseph immediately shared how each dream meant the same. Plus, he followed it with some specific advice.

Daniel interpreted several dreams for King Nebuchadnezzar of Babylon. When he heard how the king was about to execute the wise men of the empire for their inability to interpret his dream, Daniel asked to be taken to the king and stated he would give the meaning (Dan. 2:24-28). In the presence of Nebuchadnezzar, Daniel gave credit to God as the revealer and then shared the specifics of what he dreamed and its meaning.

On another occasion King Nebuchadnezzar called for Daniel. Prior to sharing the dream he made a dramatic statement concerning Daniel's ability. He recognized the "spirit of the holy gods" to be in him, thus no mystery was too great for him to interpret (4:9, 18). Notice how Daniel struggled prior to sharing the interpretation because of what was going to take place in the king's life (v. 19).

The other record of Daniel being used in interpretation is completely different. As King Belshazzar and one thousand of his nobles partied and desecrated the goblets from the temple in Jerusalem, fingers of a human hand appeared and wrote words on the palace wall. When no one could interpret them, the queen, hearing the disturbance, came into the banquet hall. She knew of Daniel and his previous interpreting of dreams. Her description was the same as Nebuchadnezzar's—"has the spirit of the holy gods in him" (5:11).

In this situation, Daniel provided a sense of double interpretation. First, he was enabled to read the words that had been inscribed. Second, he was able to show their meaning and application (see vv. 25-28).

THE MINISTRY GIFT/POSITION OF PROPHET

The Old Testament contains the life and ministry of a number of individuals, both men and women, who served God as a prophet or prophetess. Their importance is definitely emphasized by the number of individuals who fulfill this ministry position. Some of them we usually identify in other roles, but the Bible specifically states they were prophets (see Gen. 20:7; 41:25, 38; Ps. 105:15). Each of them was a human instrument by which God's word and will came to His people and other nations of the then known world.

Their calling to the task and prophetic office included a variety of settings. Moses saw the phenomenon of a bush burning without being consumed, and then God spoke to him in an audible voice (Ex. 3). Elisha was plowing when

Elijah threw his mantle around him (1 Kings 19:19-21). Before his conception, Jeremiah was selected to confront and correct Israel's unfaithfulness (Jer. 1:5). Isaiah's vision of the Lord and commissioning occurred at the temple in Jerusalem (Isa. 6). Regardless of their age or current situation at the point of their calling as a prophet, each became a spokesperson for God.

Though not a great deal of information is shared on each person, the Old Testament includes a number of prophetesses. They hold key ministry positions. Miriam, Deborah, and Huldah are in distinctly different settings while fulfilling their spiritual roles and positions as prophetess.

It's important to remember the "humanness" of the prophetic messenger. Their spiritual calling and gifting did not make them "super saints." They were physical beings subject to the normal emotions, desires, joys, and temptations. Some of them had spouses and children. Hosea faced the difficulty of an unfaithful wife. Elijah experienced fear and self-pity. Miriam fell prey to jealousy. Jonah let personal opinion get in the way of doing God's will and seeing His sovereignty.

These individuals were subject to conditions that definitely required the grace of God to endure. There was ridicule (Hos. 9:7; Jer. 20:7-8), physical discomfort and pain (1 Kings 22:24;

Jer. 20:2; 37:15-18; 38:6), demands to stop and/ or leave (Amos 7:12-13; Mic. 2:6), and death threats (Jer. 26:7-9). Though faced with such difficult circumstances, they continued to speak the Word of the Lord.

ENDNOTES

[1] Stanley M. Horton, *What the Bible Says About the Holy Spirit* (Springfield: Gospel Publishing House, 1974).

STUDY GUIDE
Chapter 3

This chapter reminded us of the active work of the Holy Spirit during the Old Testament era. Though not revealed to the extent seen in the New Testament, there are many evidences of the Spirit's working in some of the same ways as in the early church and succeeding centuries. This continuity enables us to have an expanded understanding of the operation of spiritual gifts.

Prior to reading this chapter, had you given much consideration to the active working of the Holy Spirit in the lives of Old Testament individuals and the specific events recorded? If your answer is no, you are not unusual. Many individuals assume the real work of the Holy Spirit to have begun on the Day of Pentecost.

QUESTIONS

1. What is the Holy Spirit's relationship to the other members of the Trinity?

2. Why do we see only glimpses of the Holy Spirit in the Old Testament?

3. Describe the work of the Holy Spirit in Moses' life.

4. How did the Holy Spirit work in Samson?

5. What are two gifts evident in Elisha?

6. Why was spiritual gifting necessary in the lives of Bezalel and Oholiab?

7. Which spiritual gifts did Joseph and Daniel have in common, and to whom did they minister?

8. Name three Old Testament prophetesses.

9. What are some characteristics of the prophets/prophetesses that demonstrate their "humanness"?

4

Apostles and Prophets

"It was he who gave some to be apostles, some to be prophets . . ." (Eph. 4:11).

My lunch companion said, "See those two men over there? They're apostles."

Looking across the room I saw two ordinary men, neatly dressed in suits, and enjoying the same delicious lunch as we were.

This conversation stemmed from my tablemate's presentation of a paper several hours earlier at a historical society meeting. In it he stated his denomination's position on current-day apostles. In fact, this was one of its distinctives when founded in the 1950s.

Needless to say, a follow-up question had to be asked.

"How does someone become identified as an apostle?"

"Well, we watch one's life and ministry closely. Then at some point the elders confer the designation."

Knowing this gentleman was the general overseer of his denomination, I was aware that he too was known as an apostle. However, in humility, he never mentioned it. How refreshing in a period in which individuals appear to be flaunting the title of apostle and/or prophet. But the question still remains: "Are they apostles?"

THE ISSUES

A cauldron of conflict can be the way to describe the positions on the first two ministry offices listed in Ephesians 4:11. This verse contains what is frequently referred to as the fivefold ministry. Except for the Latter Rain Movement, little attention was given to the roles of apostles and prophets within Pentecostalism. Emphasis was placed on the roles of evangelists and pastors, with some attention to the aspect of teachers. But, as a result of the events of the 1980s and 1990s, we are confronted with questions deserving our attention and careful response.

On one side are those who believe the restoration of apostles and prophets in the contemporary church provides the final step of maturing the Church (the bride of Christ) to meet Jesus (the Bridegroom) in His second coming. On the other side are those who are equally adamant in stating the office of apostle was fulfilled to completion in establishing the early church and did not continue beyond the first century.

Tucked in between these two positions are a number of other questions of considerable concern and controversy. Some of them definitely appear as heresy since there is no solid supporting biblical evidence.

1. If we accept only three of the five position gifts listed in Ephesians 4:11, how are we any different from those who believe in temporary and permanent spiritual gifts?

2. Are there apostles like those of the first century, or is it limited to apostolic ministries?

3. What are the specific roles or purposes for current-day apostles and prophets?

4. Can individuals be trained in "prophetic ministry" (schools of the prophets) that then enables them to assume the role of a prophet?

5. If there are current-day apostles and prophets, how are they to operate within a local church and denominational polity?

6. Do apostles have reservoirs of anointing that they can dispense on other believers at will?

7. Is there any biblical basis for the idea of spiritual fathers and mothers imparting their

gifts and ministries to other believers (successors)?

8. How can individuals repeatedly make "false" prophecies and still be justified as legitimate prophets?

A great number of books and articles have been written on apostles and prophets, with more still anticipated. Our discussion is limited to this one chapter. However, it is our desire to stimulate consideration of the major issues.

PROPHETIC MOVEMENT:
A HISTORICAL GLANCE

The decade of the 1980s was the emphasis period on the role and office of the prophet. No single person or event signified the beginning of this emphasis, but, rather, a number of individuals contributed to its concepts and practices.

William Branham appears to be the individual thought to be a true prophet. Though deceased for many years (1957) prior to the rise of this movement, the acceptance of his position by many in the Latter Rain Movement became a bridge to these latter ideas. Another tie was the person of Paul Cain. Cain ministered with Branham and at times took Branham's place in meetings.

Cain's birth was one of a miracle baby.

His mother, Anna, was forty-five years old and pregnant with Paul. She had heart problems, was dying from tuberculosis. She also had cancerous tumors in her breast and uterus. In answer to her prayers the Lord appeared to her in the form of an angel, touched her shoulder and said, "Daughter be of good cheer, you shall live and not die. The fruit of your womb is a male child whom I shall anoint to preach my Gospel like the apostle Paul; and you shall name him Paul."[1]

When reading of Cain's ministry there are repeated references to his predicting an earthquake that took place as well as reports of electrical surges blowing out circuits. This latter was attributed to a "heavy prophetic anointing."

Other early contributors were Kenneth Hagin and John and Paula Sanford. As early as 1959, Hagin stated the Lord Jesus appeared and anointed him to the office of prophet. In 1977, the Sanfords published *The Elijah Task: a Call to Today's Prophets*. It contained the basic tenets of the prophetic movement.

Bill Hamon continued for some thirty years to be an active promoter of the restored office of the prophet. His many books and educational efforts were extremely influential. In 1979 he began a "School of the Holy Spirit." Three years later, in 1982, Hamon began to hold prophet conferences and seminars throughout the United States and in some foreign countries. A

"School of Prophets" for training of those called to prophetic ministry was also established.

This historical glance would not be complete without mentioning the Kansas City Fellowship planted by Mike Bickle and his wife, Diane, in Kansas City, Missouri. Established in 1982, it would later become known as Metro Christian Fellowship. Four years later Grace Ministries, a parachurch organization, was organized. It represented a number of individuals in prophetic ministries with ties to the church that became known as the "Kansas City prophets." Besides Bickle, there was Paul Cain, Bob Jones, John Paul Jackson, Mike Sullivan, and David Packer.

Difficulty arose when Ernie Gruen, a Charismatic pastor from neighboring Shawnee, Kansas, released a 233-page document accusing KCF of false prophecies and outright lying. "A prophet who admits he is right only 40 percent of the time is not only a nonprophet, he is dangerous."[2]

CONCERNS WITHIN THE PROPHETIC MOVEMENT

This section provides an introductory look at some of the common concepts found within the Prophetic Movement. It is neither a complete listing nor a reflection of how the leaders may express their ideas. Provided here are some of the parameters.

Position of the prophet—Prophets are not a gift

of the Holy Spirit to the Church but rather a gift-extension of Christ himself. As a result, the prophet operates in a higher realm of ministry than do those who receive the gift of prophecy by the Holy Spirit.[3]

Prophet's role and authority—Prophets operate in a headship function within the local church. Their authority in preaching and teaching stands equal to the pastor's preaching and counseling. They, along with apostles, provide a foundation in a local church enabling maximum growth to occur.[4] Levels of authority among prophets are based on years of proven ministry.

Prophetic impartation—Two quotes summarize this view. "In ministering with prophetic anointing, it means you are enduing people with the presence of Christ and the gifts and graces of the Holy Spirit."[5] "The gift of faith operates through me and I impart the Holy Ghost by laying on of hands."[6]

Personal prophecies—Definitely at the heart of this movement is the personal prophecy where either in a private or a public setting "a word" or "words" are shared with an individual. Even though the message is to be used for confirmation rather than guidance, this principle is frequently forgotten or not known by the receiver.

Prophetic errors—This movement is very tolerant of errant prophecies. The stern warning of the Old Testament (Deut. 13:1-5) does not appear. Instead there seems to be an attitude of expecting some errors or abuses. Various reasons are offered such as allowing personal doctrine, strong convictions, prejudices, or even bitterness to color or to divert truth. Or, ". . . a prophet whose word does not come about may have simply missed what the Lord was saying in that situation."[7]

APOSTOLIC RESTORATION MOVEMENT: A HISTORICAL GLANCE

The Apostolic Restoration Movement of the 1990s appears to be a direct overflow of the prophetic emphasis of the previous decade. If there is to be a completion of the fullness of the fivefold ministry, then the role of apostle becomes a necessity. The seeming rediscovery of the prophet as part of preparing the Church included rediscovering the office of apostle. They were seen as working together as "hand and glove."

C. Peter Wagner attributes this to "hearing the Holy Spirit speaking about restoring apostles and prophets as the foundation of the church as God originally designed."[8] Previously known for his leadership in the Church Growth Movement, Wagner eventually came to the conclusion of his personally being an apostle. Later he would see himself as the presiding apostle with responsibility for developing apostolic leadership, building relationship, and providing accountability.

The term *apostolic* is seen within the early decades of Pentecostalism but with a different perspective.

> "Pentecostals, nonetheless, understood the Holy Spirit to fill them with first-century apostolic power and wisdom for a great last-day evangelization of the world. . . . though including terms like "apostolic" or "apostolic faith" in the names of their storefront missions and churches as well as on the mastheads of the periodicals.[9]

This can be seen in the environment of the Azusa Street Revival and its subsequent years. W. J. Seymour was called "apostle," but only as a title.[10] A flier prepared to share information about his Apostolic Faith Mission was titled *The Apostolic Faith Movement*. His magazine also bore the name *The Apostolic Faith*.

Another example is Florence Crawford. She received the baptism of the Holy Spirit in the initial year of the outpouring. Eventually Crawford moved to Portland, Oregon, and established a new Pentecostal denomination, The Apostolic Faith.

Not to be overlooked is the evidence of some early Pentecostal leaders believing in the reality of apostles in their day. It is suggested A. J. Tomlinson followed this view for a few years. A strong statement was presented by N. J. Holmes in his paper,

The Atomic Witness. The article, "God's Appoint-
ment," was initially published on January 8,
1912, and then republished three years later on
February 8, 1915.

> The apostleship is an office of the greatest im-
> portance and authority of all the offices con-
> ferred upon the Church. When God set the
> apostleship in the Church He did not limit
> it to the life and generation of any man. We
> find nothing in the Bible that teaches that it
> was thus limited. The office is far greater and
> more durable than the person that fills it. The
> apostleship was God's call to the man to bring
> him out to where God could put His power
> and authority upon him. It is God's office. God
> is full of apostleship and will continue to be-
> stow them when he can find the material for
> the office.[11]

After the initiation of the Latter Rain, several
smaller groups were organized around the apostolic concept. Grady R. Kent left the Church
of God of Prophecy in 1957 and founded the
Church of God (Jerusalem Acres) in Cleveland,
Tennessee; he reinstated the office of apostle and
appointed "twelve latter-day apostles" from
within his followers.[12]

The cessation concept concerning apostles
was predominant throughout Pentecostal history. Only in recent years is there a growing
number who will accept modern-day apostles.
The tremendous challenge then becomes one of

determining what qualifies a person to be considered as fulfilling this ministry position.

CONCEPTS WITHIN THE APOSTOLIC RESTORATION MOVEMENT

Apostolic need—Apostles are needed in today's Church since it has not reached perfection. The decline and mediocrity of the Church over the centuries is due to the loss of this office after the establishment in the first century. This new restoration will make up for those many lost years.

Apostolic anointing—The vacancy of apostolic anointing causes the Church to suffer. Only this anointing will enable the darkness of the world to be penetrated with the Gospel message. Apostles have a greater dimension of the Spirit's anointing than others who are called to the fivefold ministry.[13]

> Meaning it can be transferred from one person to another. This is the law of impartation. When God anoints someone, there is a measure of grace placed within that individual's life. The individual then becomes a container, or reservoir, of the anointing. . . . The Lord has chosen to use men and women as channels to release His anointing into earth.[14]

Apostolic anointing is perceived as enabling the Church to remain current and relevant within the geographical and cultural context. It also provides boldness in critical times such as persecution.

Apostolic authority—The special anointing as an apostle is also an endowment of authority and/or influence. Some suggest this authority supersedes the pastoral position within his own congregation. It is also presented as speaking on behalf of heaven. "Even the principalities and powers must acknowledge this rank because it is spiritual. They hate it and fight against it, but they cannot avoid it or overcome it."[15]

Apostolic types—The authority of an apostle is limited or operative only in the sphere of ministry to which God has assigned. As a result, apostles may be divided into various types. Some of the labels include vertical apostles, horizontal apostles, marketplace apostles, hyphenated apostles, and territorial apostles or geographic apostles.[16] There is even the thought of apostles outside of the spiritual and ecclesiastical realms in areas such as finance, government, business, and agriculture, to name a few.

Apostolic humility—Especially interesting is the projection of an apostle being a person of humility. "Genuine humility is one of the chief characteristics of an apostle. Many will question whether it is possible to exercise the extraordinary authority apostles have and still be humble. It cannot be otherwise."[17] This is perceived as being part of extraordinary character.

PROPHETS TODAY?

Yes! First, we must not be guilty of selectively choosing which of the Ephesians 4:11 ministry gifts we will allow while disallowing others. There is no evidence within Scripture that suggests the role of the prophet to be a temporary position after its founding and the outpouring of the Holy Spirit. Just the opposite is true.

1. Prophets along with apostles not only are a foundational part of establishing the early church, but they are to be a continuing part of growing and maturing the church (Eph. 3:5; 4:11-13).

2. A variety of individuals included in the Acts narratives are designated as prophets or prophetesses. They are Agabus (11:27; 21:10), prophets at Antioch (13:1), Judas and Silas (15:32), and Philip's four daughters (21:9).

3. The words of Jesus indicate the functioning of prophets within the Church body. In Matthew 10:41 He said those who receive a prophet will receive a prophet's reward. Mark records Jesus' warning against false prophets, which assumes the existence of true prophets (13:22).

4. In the second century there are evidences of prophets and the prophetic ministry. *The Didache* or *Teaching of the Apostles* included specific guidelines

to determine a true or false prophet and how they were to be treated. Not to be forgotten is the movement known as Montanism with its emphasis on prophecy, prophets, and prophetesses.

5. The absence of recognizing the office of prophet over many centuries is not proof in itself of the cessation of this ministry gift. Keep in mind how important basic biblical doctrines have been suppressed only to rise in a time of spiritual renewal and spiritually invigorated leadership.

Yes, there are prophets today! We must not allow the abuses of some sincerely wrong believers and the existence of false prophets to blind or to rob us of what God intends for His church. This does, however, place on us the responsibility of determining a true prophet. Two qualifications found in Deuteronomy provide the foundation.

1. *Faithfulness to God's Word* (Deut. 13)—This can be seen in two areas. The prophet's message must harmonize and totally agree with the written Scriptures. Any deviation from the basic truth disqualifies the message. The other area is the prophet's lifestyle, which must be lived within the directives of Christian morality and integrity as presented in the Bible.

2. *Fulfillment of prophecies* (Deut. 18:21-22)— Unless prophecies are fulfilled within their

context (person, location, time period) the person is not a prophet. The old saying of "The proof is in the pudding" applies here. The true prophet doesn't offer generalities that common sense knows to be true. Consider this one as an example: "There are a number of you here tonight or in my listening audience with knee problems, and God wants to bring wholeness to you." In any general populace there are a number of people with knee problems ranging from the general wear of aging to the many athletic-related injuries.

Accepting the position of prophet doesn't automatically give the prophet free reign within a local church. The prophet must not be allowed to undermine the pastor's authority and responsibility to shepherd the flock. Neither should prophets be allowed to speak in a manner which produces unnecessary division within the body. Great care needs to be exercised if inviting a transient prophet into one's church. Continued care should be given to keep a resident prophet close to the pastor.

APOSTLES TODAY?

Yes. However, this response in the positive is with careful qualification.

The beginning point centers on the meaning behind the term *apostle*. Basically, it means one who is sent with specific purpose or commission. Ancient Greeks used it . . .

> . . . to describe leaders sent to colonize areas.
> These leaders had control of and authority over
> sculling vessels that carried people and cargo to
> expand the empire. It also described someone
> who was sent as an ambassador or envoy with
> authority based on the authority of the sender.[18]

Christ's selection of the Twelve clearly fits within this definition. Often they are referred to as the unique apostles or even the college of apostles due to their being the foundational leaders of the Church. Through them and the apostle Paul the New Testament was written and the expansion of the Church undertaken.

We must not overlook the distinct qualifications of this initial group. They were witnesses to the life, death, and resurrection of Jesus. This becomes evident when choosing someone to fill the vacancy of Judas Iscariot (see Acts 1:21-22). Having seen Jesus was emphasized by Paul as he defended his apostleship (1 Cor. 9:1). The evidence of signs, wonders, and miracles are another clear mark of an apostle (2 Cor. 12:12).

Others besides the Twelve and the apostle Paul are called apostles and fulfill the definition of being sent. Andronicus and Junias, relatives of Paul, were described as apostles in the list of greetings sent to the church in

Rome (Rom. 16:7). Paul included James, the Lord's brother, in the designation of apostle (Gal. 1:19). In Paul's Epistle to the Thessalonians, he reminded them of his and Silas' first visit to the city. In the process he included his ministry partner in the designation of apostle (1 Thess. 2:6). Paul also referred to Epaphroditus and others as apostles in the original language of the Scriptures, though translators use terms such as *representatives* or *messengers* (2 Cor. 8:23; Phil. 2:25).

So, what conclusions do we come to in light of this information?

One choice is to believe after the end of the Twelve's ministry all others are part of apostolic ministries. This stems from there being no New Testament basis for the succession of apostles beyond the first century. They were in a unique role which cannot be duplicated.

The other choice is to believe in the continuance of the ministry office of apostle. Foundational apostles established the Church with continuing leaders exercising the same ministry of evangelism, church planting, and leadership.

We choose the latter. In doing so, tremendous care needs to be taken to not exalt the title. Just because someone claims the title doesn't make the statement true! The key is the ministry fruit and the individual's personal life. Not to be overlooked is the issue of accountability.

There are some specific qualifications for anyone to be even considered as a modern-day apostle.

1. Humility dominates as they genuinely love and serve people.

2. Signs, wonders, and miracles are evident in their sphere of ministry.

3. Financial relationships are handled with wisdom and personal integrity (see 2 Cor. 11:7-12).

4. Christian ministry is being established among the unevangelized as they are brought to salvation and discipleship.

5. The authority and covering of the church (denomination, fellowship) is valued. (Notice the various times the apostles reported to the church.)

6. Ministry constantly dominates while personal glory is shunned and the title rarely used.

7. Sacrifice is expected and willingly encountered even to the point of death.

In light of this listing there are several conclusions to be offered. First, throughout the history of the Christian church there have been individuals who met these qualifications but never even thought of the title. Second, there are individuals today laboring in the Kingdom without fanfare or recognition who truly are apostles. Third, some people recklessly claim the title but definitely fail to meet the qualifications.

Consider the following quote as an excellent summarization.

And, yes, there are apostles abroad today who are carrying out the same mission as the apostles in the New Testament. Who are they? The nearest parallel to the New Testament and historic use of the term "apostle" are those missionaries—often unnamed, untouched—who are bringing the message of the Gospel for the first time to previously unreached people and tribes. They are busy translating the Scriptures and planting churches where none existed.[19]

Some of these "missionaries" are working in the inner cities of major cities of the world. They aren't seen on TBN. They aren't the featured speakers at conventions and seminars. They aren't pictured in the major Christian periodicals. They aren't flaunting the title. But they are spreading the Gospel— unheralded and unsung.

ENDNOTES

[1] Pytches, *Some Say it Thundered*, 22.

[2] Pytches, *Some Say it Thundered*, 146.

[3] Bill Hamon, *Prophets and Personal Prophecy* (Shippenberg: Destiny Image Publisher, Inc., 1987) 51-52.

[4] Hamon, *Prophets and Personal Prophecy*, 52-53.

[5] Bill Hamon, *Prophets, Pitfalls and Principles* (Shippenberg: Destiny Image Publisher, Inc., 1987) 196.

[6] Kenneth Hagin, *The Holy Spirit and His Gifts* (Tulsa: Rhema Bible Church, 1974) 89.

[7] Doug Beacham, *Rediscovering the Role of Apostles and Prophets* (Franklin Springs: Life Springs Resources, 2004) 147.

[8] Global Harvest Ministries: Yesterday, Today and Tomorrow! Online <*http://www.globalharvest.org/index.asp?action=about*>. Retrieved July 11, 2005.

[9] Edgar R. Lee, ed., *He Gave Apostles: Apostolic Ministry in the 21st Century* (Springfield: Assemblies of God Theological Seminary, 2005) 7-8.

[10] Beacham, *Rediscovering the Role of Apostles and Prophets*, 34.

[11] Beacham, *Rediscovering the Role of Apostles and Prophets*, 53.

[12] Wade H. Philips, "Apostle, Apostolic" in *Encyclopedia of Pentecostal and Charismatic Christianity*, ed. by Stanley M. Burgess (New York: Routledge, 2006) 39.

[13] Eckhardt, *Moving in the Apostolic*, 25.

[14] Eckhardt, *Moving in the Apostolic*, 102-03.

[15] Eckhardt, *Moving in the Apostolic*, 43.

[16] C. Peter Wagner, *Apostles and Prophets: The Foundation of the Church* (Venture: Regal Books, 2000) 40, 43, 46, 52.

[17] C. Peter Wagner, *Churchquake* (Venturia: Regal Books, 1999) 118.

[18] Beacham, *Rediscovering the Role of Apostles and Prophets*, 1323.

[19] Vincent Synan, "Apostles Today?" in Lee, *He Gave Apostles: Apostolic Ministry in the 21st Century*, 23.

STUDY GUIDE
Chapter 4

Nowhere in Scripture do we find evidence supporting the cessation of apostles and prophets. These ministry gift offices are needed in the Church while it is being fully unified in faith and matured. New believers, regretfully, may stray from truth and commitment. They need to be returned to their previous relationship. At times whole organizations decline and they too need to hear the voices of rebuke and restoration.

Prior to reading this chapter what were your views on current-day apostles and prophets? Have your views changed in any way? If yes, what are the specifics?

QUESTIONS

1. Who are some of the contributing individuals to the Prophetic Movement?

2. What are the five basic concepts in the Prophetic Movement?

3. How widespread is the cessation concept of apostles within Pentecostal history?

4. What are the five basic concepts in the Apostolic Restoration Movement?

5. Who were some of the prophets ministering in the early church?

6. What are the two qualifications for prophets found in Deuteronomy?

7. What is the meaning of the term *apostle*?

8. Who is listed in Scripture with the designation of apostle besides the Twelve?

9. List seven qualifications for a modern-day apostle.

5

Evangelists, Pastors, and Teachers

Ephesians 4:7-16

Are evangelists really needed since times have changed and people do not have time to attend extended meetings? Has the basic role of the pastor changed? Where does the teacher fit? Evangelists, pastors, and teachers are not ingenious creations of the world or of the Church—they are gifts of the triumphant, exalted Christ to His church. These ministers are given as part of His provisions for His body, His church, so that it can become what He intends it to become.

The Book of Ephesians emphasizes the Church as a creation of God's grace. We have been brought from death to life, from "no people" to

"God's people," from hopelessness to hope, from "far off" to "near," and from separated to reconciled. The Church is God's workmanship, His work of art, His masterpiece created in Christ Jesus (Eph. 2:10). This masterpiece is evident for the entire world to see. To the cosmic realm (the spiritual forces against God), the church is a display of multifaceted divine wisdom (3:10). The Church is not an afterthought, but it is part of God's divine purpose in His Son, Jesus Christ, through whom we have freedom of access to the Triune God (vv. 11-12). The Church is a work of the Triune God: one Spirit, one Lord, and one God and Father (4:5-6). Since we by grace are part of God's new creation, we are challenged to conduct our daily lives, by grace, in a way that is worthy of the calling to which we have been called (4:1). In order to help the Church to achieve God's eternal purposes, Christ gave apostles, prophets, evangelists, pastors, and teachers.

Paul[1] began this section (vv. 7-16) by declaring that God's grace was given to each of us according to the measure of Christ's gift. He then quoted from Psalm 68:18. Psalm 68 celebrates an occurrence (perhaps the return of the ark of the covenant to Israel) in which the Lord Jehovah has triumphed over His enemies. The picture is painted of a king's returning from battle and ascending the mountain with his train of captives and the spoils of war. The psalm reminds God's people of His rescuing them from their enemies and preserving them in the wilderness wanderings. God Jehovah overcomes every enemy and establishes His kingdom. As a messianic psalm, not only is a present event celebrated, but a greater fulfillment is anticipated.

Paul viewed the ultimate fulfillment in the Christ-event. Christ first descended from heaven in the Incarnation. He further humbled Himself to death on the cross and His body was buried (note Phil. 2:5-11). Paul emphasized that this is the same Jesus who ascended. The resurrection of Jesus is a reality. He obtained complete victory. He who rose victoriously ascended into the heavens and "far above all the heavens, that He might fill all things" (Eph. 4:10 NKJV). F. F. Bruce elaborated, ". . . that He might pervade the whole universe with His presence, from the lowest depths to the highest heights . . . that is why His people can now enjoy His immediate presence simultaneously, wherever they may be, whereas in the days of His flesh He could only be in one place at one time."[2] Philippians 2:9 says, "Therefore God also has highly exalted Him and given Him the name which is above every name" (NKJV). Paul viewed Jesus' death on the cross as the pivotal victory. In Colossians 2:15, written about the same time as Ephesians, he said, "He disarmed rulers and authorities and made a public example of them, triumphing over them in it." (Also note Heb. 2:14-15; 1 John 3:8.) The Resurrection and Ascension were inevitable results of Jesus' triumph on the cross.

How does Paul's statement "and he gave gifts to his people" (Eph. 4:8b) relate to Psalm 68:18, which pictures the king as receiving gifts from others? After discussing various possibilities, George Stoeckhardt concluded that Paul intended to quote only the first part of Psalm 68:18, ending with "He led a host of captives."

> To every Christian, grace is given according to the measure of the gift of Christ. In order to accomplish this, Christ, as the psalm states, ascended on high, leading captivity captive. This triumphant ascension was in reality the foundation and prerequisite for the granting and bestowing of gifts. After quoting the psalm . . . Paul returns to his chief statement v. 7: and so after his ascension, which was at the same time His triumph over His enemies, and in virtue of this ascension, He gave gifts to men.[3]

F. F. Bruce believed that Paul quoted the Syriac version of the Old Testament (the Peshitta).

> The original picture is of a victorious king ascending the mountain of the Lord in triumphal procession, attended by a long train of captives, receiving tribute from his new subjects (according to the one reading) and bestowing largesse upon the crowds which line his processional

> route (according to the second reading). For
> Paul's present purpose, the reading which
> speaks of the conqueror as *giving* gifts is more
> appropriate than that which speaks of him
> as *receiving* them . . . but the ascended Christ
> may well be pictured as receiving from His Fa-
> ther the gifts which He proceeded to bestow
> among men.[4]

We may also note that Psalm 68 ends with "He gives power and strength to his people" (v. 35), so there is no contradiction, whatever the reading.

The triumphant Christ made full provision through His gifts of grace to His church. He gave a variety of ministers to His church to equip His people to accomplish His purposes. Apostles and prophets have been discussed, so we will now turn our attention to the evangelists, pastors, and teachers.

EVANGELISTS

The noun *evangelist* is found only three times in the New Testament. Paul instructed Timothy to "do the work of an evangelist" (2 Tim. 4:5). Philip, whose four daughters were prophets, was called an evangelist (Acts 21:8). The third instance is in Ephesians 4:11.

The verb *evangelize* is a prominent word in the New Testament. Evangelizing is proclaiming the good news. It is often translated as "preach."

An example of this is in Acts 8:4, where the word *evangelizing* is translated "preaching the word" (NKJV). Another example is in Luke 4:18, where the term *evangelize the poor* is translated "to preach the good news to the poor."

The "Evangel" (the Gospel) is the "good news" (see Rom. 1:16). The evangelist evangelizes with the Evangel!

It is expected that all of God's people be involved in proclaiming the good news of Jesus Christ. There are those, however, whom Christ has called and gifted whom He then gives to the Church as part of the equipping ministers. In the account in Acts 8, persecutions drove many Christians out of Jerusalem and into Judea and Samaria. The apostles remained in Jerusalem. Acts 8:4 says, "Now those who were scattered went from place to place, proclaiming the word." Evangelizing was the work of the people of God. The next verse says, "Then Philip went down to the city of Samaria and preached Christ to them" (v. 5 NKJV). Philip, the evangelist who had been chosen earlier to serve on the seven-member benevolent board, was now actively engaged in evangelizing.

Philip's preaching was accompanied by signs, healings, and deliverances from demon possession. Multitudes listened and heeded, and there was much joy in the city. Many in the city had lived under the bondage of Simon the sorcerer, but "when they believed Philip as he preached the good news of the kingdom of God and the name of Jesus Christ, they were baptized, both men and women" (v. 12). Philip, the evangelist, was Christ's gift to the Church. His ministry was not operated independently. The apostles Peter and John came and prayed for these who "had received the word of God" that they would receive the Holy Spirit (vv. 14-17 NKJV). This activity demonstrates the cooperative efforts of Christ's gifts to His church.

As Christ has given this minister (evangelist) to the Church, He also directs him. The angel of the Lord first directed Philip to "go toward the south along the road which goes down from Jerusalem to Gaza" (v. 26 NKJV). Philip obeyed and went. He saw a chariot, and "the Spirit said to Philip, 'Go over to this chariot and join it'" (v. 29). Philip obeyed and ran to the chariot and heard the man reading aloud from Isaiah the prophet. With wisdom, Philip asked if he understood what he was reading and the man responded, "How can I, unless someone guides me?" (v. 31). The man then invited Philip to sit with him. The man was reading from Isaiah 53, and he posed the question to Philip, "About whom, may I ask you, does the prophet say this, about himself or about someone else?" (Acts 8:34). "Then Philip opened his mouth, and beginning at this Scripture, preached Jesus to him" (v. 35 NKJV). The Ethiopian believed, accepted the Gospel, and was baptized in water by Philip. Then the Ethiopian "went on his way rejoicing" (vv. 36-39 NKJV). The Spirit of the Lord seized Philip and "Philip found himself at Azotus, and as he was passing through the region, he proclaimed the good news to all the towns until he came to Caesarea" (v. 40). It was in Caesarea where Paul found him later and stayed several days with him and his family (21:8). This is another instance that demonstrates Philip's connection to the Church.

Since Philip is the only person who was actually called an evangelist in the New Testament, we accept him as our basic model of an evangelist. An evangelist is of highest spiritual character, respected by others, and full of the Holy Spirit and wisdom. The evangelist's basic message is proclaiming the good news of Jesus Christ and the kingdom of God. The basic goal is to bring unbelievers to faith in and commitment to Jesus Christ. This involves public confession in water baptism, which should also connect them to other believers.

The evangelist has a sensitivity to the Holy Spirit and a prompt obedience to His direction. The evangelist is intent on sharing the Gospel whether in mass evangelism or personal evangelism. There is a burden to see the lost ones saved.

The evangelist serves as part of the spiritual team to bring Christ's church to its intended maturity. The fact that Philip had four daughters who prophesied seems to indicate that Philip did not neglect his own family while evangelizing others. This should be an example to evangelists today to nurture their own families in the faith.

The Church needs to reaffirm the call of evangelists and to appreciate the evangelist as a gift of Christ to the Church. We need to receive the ministry of the evangelists and assist and cooperate with the fulfilling of their ministry. Approaches change and methodologies change, but Christ's gift of evangelists remains. The responsibility to fulfill this giftedness rests with the evangelists and the rest of the Church.

When the evangelist is understood in the context of Ephesians 4 and is seen as part of the spiritual team to equip others and bring the Church to maturity, perhaps more attention could be given to the evangelist's working with, in, and through a local church. In this way, the evangelist could train and guide persons in the local church in evangelistic ministry; the team could find creative ways to evangelize the city; and the evangelist and team could go periodically to other places to conduct evangelistic ministries.

PASTORS AND TEACHERS

Christ has given pastors to His church. The word for "pastor" is *shepherd*. The shepherd feeds, nurtures, guides, and disciplines the sheep. In the Old Testament, God condemned many of the spiritual shepherds who cared for themselves rather than caring for the sheep; who ran when the sheep were threatened; who did not lead the sheep; and who destroyed and scattered the sheep (Jer. 23:1-2; Ezek. 34:1-10). God promises that He himself will become the Shepherd of His sheep:

> I myself will be the shepherd of my sheep, and I will make them lie down, says the Lord God. I will seek the lost, and I will bring back the strayed, and I will bind up the injured, and I will strengthen the weak, but the fat and the strong I will destroy. I will feed them with justice (Ezek. 34:15-16). I will raise up shepherds over them who will shepherd them, and they shall not fear any longer, or be dismayed, nor shall any be missing, says the Lord (Jer. 23:4).

Jesus Christ is the Good Shepherd, the One who ultimately fulfills God's promises concerning the shepherd. Jesus proclaimed, "I am the good shepherd. The good shepherd lays down his life for the sheep" (John 10:11). He is referred to as "our Lord Jesus, that great Shepherd of the sheep" (Heb. 13:20); He is called "the shepherd and guardian of your souls" (1 Peter 2:25) and "the Chief Shepherd" (5:4).

When Jesus reinstated and recommissioned Simon, He told him, "Feed my lambs" (John 21:15), "Shepherd my little sheep" (v. 16 Gr. Trans.), and "Feed my little sheep" (v. 17 Gr. Trans.). Simon Peter is commissioned to fulfill a pastoral role. The term *pastor* became interchangeably used with *elder*. Simon Peter identified himself as an elder as he gave instructions to elders.

> Tend the flock of God that is in your charge, exercising the oversight, not under compulsion but willingly, as God would have you do it—not for sordid gain but eagerly. Do not lord it over those in your charge, but be examples to the flock. And when the chief shepherd appears, you will win the crown of glory that never fades away (1 Peter 5:2-4).

Paul charged the Ephesian elders:

> Keep watch over yourselves and over all the flock, of which the Holy Spirit has made you overseers, to shepherd the church of God that he obtained with the blood of his own Son. I know that after I have gone, savage wolves will come in among you, not sparing the flock. Some even of your own group will come distorting the truth in order to entice the disciples to follow them. Therefore be alert, remembering that for three years I did not cease night or day to warn everyone with tears (Acts 20:28-31).

Some of the responsibilities of the pastors/elders can be seen from these verses. Pastors are to

shepherd the flock. Pastors are to oversee willingly and eagerly with pure motives. Pastors are
to lead by example, not as dictators. Pastors are
to stay alert to dangers and guard the flock from
savage wolves. Pastors are to realize that the
Church is God's church, purchased by the blood
of Jesus Christ. Pastors also should realize the
ultimate accountability is to Christ, and the ultimate reward is from Christ, the Chief Shepherd.

The terms *elder* and *overseer* are also used interchangeably in the New Testament (note Acts 14:23;
20:17; 1 Tim. 4:14; 5:17, 19; Titus 1:5, 7; 1 Peter 5:1,
5; James 5:14). The primary qualification of a pas-
tor/elder/overseer is to be "above reproach" (1
Tim. 3:2). Christian character is paramount. These
Christian qualities are further explicated by Paul
in 1 Timothy 3. Paul also said that the pastor/elder/
overseer must be "able to teach" (v. 2 NKJV). Even
though every pastor needs to teach, there are some
who give special labor to preaching and teaching
while leading the flock. "Let the elders who rule
well be considered worthy of double honor, especially those who labor in preaching and teaching"
(5:17).

Before each of these gifted ministers listed in
Ephesians 4:11, there is a definite article, except
before "teachers." Does this indicate that pastors and teachers are the same persons? The
opinions are divided on this issue.

> The omission of the article from *teachers* seems to indicate that pastors and teachers are included under one class. The two belong together. No man is fit to be a pastor who cannot also teach, and the teacher needs the knowledge which pastoral experience teaches.[5]

Those holding this view could translate the terms as "teaching shepherd" or "pastor-teacher." A different view was given by Andrew Lincoln:

> It is more likely that they were overlapping functions, but that while almost all pastors were also teachers, not all teachers were also pastors. Whether the two functions were performed by a single individual within a particular local situation may well have depended on what gifted persons were present in that situation. The one definite article is therefore best taken as suggesting this close association of functions between two types of ministers who both operate within the local congregation.[6]

It seems that the close relationship of pastoring and teaching is emphasized: while the pastor must be a teacher, the teacher must be pastoral in teaching. A good example is the Rabbi who did not give verbal lessons only. He daily lived out what He taught and led the students in discovering truth. Jesus, this supreme example of the shepherd/teacher relationship, called His disciples to be with Him. In their day-to-day living, He related to them by precept and example the lessons of the kingdom of God. He guided and guarded the disciples as He prepared them to receive His ultimate sacrifice.

Not only is the gift of teacher listed in Ephesians 4, but teaching is listed in the spiritual gifts in 1 Corinthians 12:28 and Romans 12:7. Acts 13:1 says that there were prophets and teachers in the church at Antioch. The Word of God indicates that the teacher has been placed in the body of Christ.

> Such people have a special God-given gift that enables them to explain, expound and proclaim the Word of God with power for the purpose of enlightening and building up the fellowship of believers. Endowed by the Spirit for the task of teaching, they are able to relate Scripture to the immediate needs of the congregation. This task requires them to hold on to the faithful Word so that they can give instruction in sound doctrine and offer an effective defense for their beliefs (Titus 1:9).[7]

Ephesians 4:12 indicates that the apostles, prophets, evangelists, pastors, and teachers are Christ's gifts to the Church for equipping the saints to the work of ministry, to the building up of the body of Christ. These ministries continue in order to enable the Body to attain unity of the faith and knowledge of the Son of God to attain maturity. Further, these ministries help the people of God to recognize and resist deceitful doctrines and schemes and to continue to grow

up in every way. This growth is demonstrated
by the Church's speaking the truth in love and
upbuilding itself in love (Eph. 4:13-16).

ENDNOTES

[1] The authorship of Ephesians is disputed, but I accept Paul as the author.

[2] F. F. Bruce, *The Epistle to the Ephesians* (Old Tappan, NJ: Fleming H. Revell, 1961) 84.

[3] George Stoeckhardt (Tr. Martin S. Sommer), *Ephesians* (St. Louis: Concordia, 1952) 194.

[4] F. F. Bruce, op. cit., 82.

[5] M. R. Vincent, *Word Studies in the New Testament* (Wilmington, Delaware: Associated Publishers and Authors, 1972) 858.

[6] Andrew T. Lincoln, *Word Biblical Commentary (Ephesians)* vol. 42 (Nashville: Thomas Nelson Publishers, 1990) 250.

[7] French L. Arrington, *Encountering the Holy Spirit*, 295.

STUDY GUIDE
Chapter 5

For the equipping, maturing, and growing in the body of Christ, the Lord has provided gifted ministers as His gifts to the Church. These ministers work together as a spiritual team to help the Church to carry out its eternal purpose.

QUESTIONS

1. Compare and contrast the following terms: evangelist, evangelizing, and evangel.

2. List the three locations of the word *evangelist* in the New Testament.

3. How does Paul use the quotation from Psalm 68:18 in the Ephesians passage?

4. Discuss the use of the imagery of "shepherd" from the Old Testament and the New Testament.

5. What are the differences and similarities in pastors and teachers?

6

Introduction to the Charismata

1 Corinthians 12:1-3

Many churches today have well-trained staff members. These individuals know how to communicate; they know how to lead. Many of these individuals are well-researched, rehearsed, and rather refined. Do they need the gifts of the Spirit within their operation, or can they do it alone? Do we need the supernatural enablement of the Holy Spirit? The answer is "Yes!" We, as members, need to understand the gifts of the Spirit in order to make ourselves available to God to be used by Him. The challenges faced by the Church today are greater than our cumulative abilities and wisdom can meet.

Perhaps you have heard individuals bemoan the fact that the gifts are not operative as they once were or as these persons think they should be. Perhaps individuals ask the questions, "Where are the gifts? Why don't we see them operative anymore?" A better question would be "What can I do to offer myself to God to be used by Him in the exercise of spiritual gifts?"

God has created human beings with astonishing capacities for learning, creativity, and challenging accomplishments. Human capabilities and energies to make and sell products and to offer services are marvelous. Human accomplishments are astonishing!

However, when considering spiritual things, we realize that the needs exceed our human capacity. The needs exceed our human wisdom, our human power, and our human ability. We need spiritual gifts in addition to what *we* can contribute.

There are many things that we can do and that we should do, and yet, if we are limited merely by our human abilities, we could be no more than a social group getting together or a welfare agency doing its work. We realize, however, that the Holy Spirit has called us together as the body of Christ and that it is imperative to have divine energy and direction to fulfill His will.

The Scripture tells us in 2 Timothy 3:7 that in the last days people will be ever learning and never arriving at truth. We live in an age of an explosion of knowledge, and yet, we realize there is a limitation to human knowledge. It takes the Holy Spirit to reveal divine truth to us. We need the work of the Holy Spirit within us. Jesus said that when the Holy Spirit comes, He will guide us into all truth. We need Him to lead us beyond mere human capabilities and beyond human categories of learning that we might achieve truth. Sometimes, knowledge is confusing, and we must depend upon the Holy Spirit to help us discern what *real* truth is all about.

We face situations in the Church when, despite our knowledge and experience, we don't know what to do. We need supernatural wisdom in those situations. We need Him to help us have wisdom that is beyond human ability in order to discern how we ought to respond. Many times we face issues which need power beyond our own. In those times, we need a supernatural endowment of power.

The Lord Jesus has given us the commission to evangelize the world, to share the Gospel with every human being in the world. With all the human technology, this challenge still is beyond our grasp, except in the power of the Holy Spirit. We need His supernatural empowerment

so that barriers will come down and He can communicate the Gospel of Christ through us and
beyond us to all the world. Mere human words
cannot bring conviction to the human heart. It is
the Holy Spirit who brings conviction, for Jesus
has said, as recorded in John 16, that He will con-
vince the unbelievers of sin and righteousness
and judgment. We need His supernatural endowment in order to evangelize the lost.

When individuals come to Jesus Christ and
acknowledge Him as Savior and Lord, these
individuals need to become matured in the
Body. And yet, there's a limitation to what we
can do in that maturing process. We need the
Holy Spirit's involvement with us so the body
of Christ will be built up. These are some of the
reasons we need the gifts of the Spirit operative.
Beyond these reasons, the very fact that God has
provided the gifts of the Spirit for His church
is reason enough in itself to say, "We need the
gifts of the Spirit." Why would He have provided these gifts of the Spirit for the Church if they
were not needed? For what reason do they exist
if we do not need the gifts of the Spirit?

SPIRITUAL GIFTS/CHARISMATA

Paul began his discussion of spiritual gifts
by saying, "Now concerning spiritual gifts,
brothers and sisters, I do not want you to be

uninformed" (1 Cor. 12:1). The word translated
"spiritual gifts" could also be translated "spiritual persons." The context indicates "spiritual gifts"
to be the preferred translation.[1] On the formula
"I do not want you to be ignorant" (which Paul
also used in 1 Corinthians 10:1; 1 Thessalonians
4:13; 2 Corinthians 1:8; Romans 1:13; and Romans
11:25), Fee commented, "Paul almost certainly
does not intend to give new information, but an
additional slant, or a corrective, to their understanding of 'the things of the Spirit.'"[2]

In 1 Corinthians 12:4, Paul used another word
for gifts, the word *charismaton* which means
"grace gifts." The terms *spiritual gifts* and *grace
gifts* are used interchangeably, but with a difference in emphasis. The term *spiritual gifts* emphasizes that it is the Spirit who originates, distributes, and directs *all* of these gifts. The term *grace
gifts* emphasizes that no one ever earns or deserves these gifts; they are gifts of divine favor.
The chapter begins with *spiritual gifts*, continues
in verse 4 with *grace gifts*, and ends in verse 31
with *grace gifts*. 1 Corinthians 14:1 follows with
spiritual gifts. This usage demonstrates the inter-
changeable nature of the different terms.

The Holy Spirit is involved in every operation
of the ministry of the Church—from the time
of the conviction of an individual, to the time
an individual makes full confession of Jesus as

Lord, until the time people are being edified in even more spectacular ways. So from the less spectacular—the confession that Jesus is Lord—to the more spectacular—some of the other operations of the gifts of the Spirit—the Holy Spirit is involved in every operation of the church of the living God. The work of the Holy Spirit does not glorify individual person-alities in the Church; the Holy Spirit glorifies Jesus Christ. When we talk about the gifts of the Spirit, we are not talking about the gifts be-ing operative so we can glory in the gifts, not so we can testify of how great the gifts are in our church, not so that we can glory in individ-uals who are used by God in the operation of the gifts, but we glory in the fact Jesus is Lord. Holy Spirit giftedness in operation will testify to the fact that Jesus is Lord.

The Holy Spirit has chosen to inform us concerning spiritual gifts. He has informed us about the diversity of spiritual gifts operated in the unity of the body of Christ. He has in-formed us about the origin and Distributor of the gifts. The Holy Spirit desires that we devel-op an appreciation of each gift and have pure motives in our desire for spiritual gifts. The Holy Spirit wants us to be informed about the proper operation of spiritual gifts, and He de-sires that we be fully informed about spiritual gifts so we can participate with joy and freedom in all of God's provisions for His people.

Note the following comments about whether these gifts are for the Body today. Gordon Fee said that many would conclude that these gifts are not for today.

> However, there has been a spate of literature whose singular urgency has been to justify the limiting of these gifts to the first-century church. It is fair to say of this literature that its authors have found what they were looking for and have thereby continued to reject such manifestation in the Church. It can also be fairly said that such rejection is not exegetically based, but results in every case, from a prior hermeneutical and theological commitment.[3]

Fee continued:

> Perhaps the greater tragedy for the Church is that it should have lost such touch with the Spirit of God in its ongoing life that it should settle for what is only ordinary and thus feel the urgency to justify itself in this way.[4]

May God help us not to be guilty of settling for what is ordinary. We cannot settle for our accumulated wisdom or knowledge. We need what is extraordinary! We need the gift of wisdom operative in our Church in the body of believers.

As we consecrate and seek God for His gifts to be operative as He has designed them, then and only then can we accomplish everything within the will of God for the Church. It is not by might, and it is not by power, but it is by the Spirit of the living God that the Church can become all that God intends it to be.

ENDNOTES

[1] The word can be either masculine (spiritual persons) or neuter (spiritual gifts or things of the Spirit).

[2] Gordon Fee, *The First Epistle to the Corinthians* (Grand Rapids: William B. Eerdmans Publishing Company, 1987) 576.

[3] *Ibid.*, 600.

[4] *Ibid.*

STUDY GUIDE
Chapter 6

In this day of spiritual confusion and spiritual ignorance, God's people need to be informed about all His provisions. In relationship to spiritual gifts, we need to know what God's Word says.

QUESTIONS

1. Are spiritual gifts available today?

2. List three reasons spiritual gifts are needed today.

3. What are the major emphases in the terms *spiritual gifts* and *charismata*?

4. According to 1 Corinthians 12:1-3, how can we discern the legitimacy of a spiritual manifestation?

7

Instructive Proclamation

There are various lists of spiritual gifts. Paul identified nine gifts in 1 Corinthians. Each is a spiritual endowment. Each is a direct operation of the Holy Spirit through the life of a human being. Though we don't understand everything concerning spiritual gifts, God desires for us to develop a sufficient understanding in order to see these gifts operative in the body of Christ. Paul had said to the Corinthian church that they are not lacking in any spiritual gift. To this same group, he says, however, that he does not want them to be ignorant concerning the spiritual gifts.

We also need to understand as much as we can about spiritual gifts so that we can accept His operation in and through our lives for the benefit of the Body. You may say, "This is not applicable to me because God would never operate a spiritual

gift in my life." Are you open to His doing it?
Do you desire for Him to operate the spiritual
gifts in the Body? Do you want Him to operate
in your life? If, indeed, we want Him to operate
spiritual gifts in the Body, then why should we
not be asking, "Lord, is it I that you desire to
use in the spiritual gifts?" Do we simply stand
on the sideline and complain that the gifts are
not operative, when we ourselves are not conse-
crating and seeking God for the operation of the
gifts in and through our lives individually? It is
for the *common* good.

One of the questions that arises is "Are these
gifts given to individuals, or are they simply in
the Body to be operated by the Holy Spirit?" It
is true that there are individuals through whom
the Holy Spirit chooses to operate certain spiritual gifts more frequently. For example, it is apparent according to 1 Corinthians 14 that some
persons are known by a congregation as inter-
preters of tongues because the Holy Spirit ordinarily operates this gift through them. Paul said
that if the interpreter is not present, the speaker
in other tongues should pray for an interpretation. So the operation of the spiritual gift is not
just dependent upon the presence of certain individuals. No one owns the spiritual gift. It is
owned by God himself. The gift is operated by
the Holy Spirit. It is assigned by and allotted

by the Spirit of God to consecrated individuals for the benefit of everybody. Each time the gift is operative, it is under the jurisdiction of the Holy Spirit. It is not given to anyone to operate at will.

The Spirit of the Lord does not take control of, or commandeer, anyone in the operation of the spiritual gift. He is a God who desires to operate as you submit to Him, as you cooperate with Him. On the other hand, evil spirits sometimes take charge of people to say things and do things. These people cannot help themselves. That is not the way it is with the gifts of the Spirit. So, if you are waiting for Him to take charge of you, to stand you up and do something through you, you are waiting in vain. He desires our submission and cooperation with Him. As He operates the gift in us, we have to trust Him and rely upon Him. We need to be close enough to Him so that we can submit to Him and cooperate with what the Spirit is doing in our lives.

THE WORD OF WISDOM

The gift of the word of wisdom could be translated as a "message" of wisdom, a "discourse" of wisdom, a "declaration" of wisdom, or a "proclamation" of wisdom. Both the word of wisdom and the word of knowledge give instructions to the congregation. Much is said about wisdom in Scripture. There is a body of material called Wisdom Literature: Job, Proverbs, et cetera. Wisdom Literature is a result of individuals' attempts to understand how human nature works, how God operates, and how human beings should deal with questions such as "Why do bad things happen to good people?"

In the Proverbs, wisdom is the principal thing (4:7). The fear of the Lord is the beginning of wisdom (9:10). Proverbs 8 says that wisdom cries in the streets, seeking for people to give attention to it. Individuals can attain wisdom. As a matter of fact, Proverbs 29:15 says that the rod and reproof bring wisdom, showing that sometimes we learn wisdom from our parents by discipline that we receive. Sometimes it comes by the help of others; sometimes through experience itself.

Wisdom is certainly needed. James 1:5 says that if any lacks wisdom, let that person ask of God—a God who gives liberally and does not upbraid you—and you will receive that wisdom. In James 3:13 and following, James discusses the differences in godly wisdom and human wisdom. Paul also did the same thing in 1 Corinthians 1-3. In these chapters, the word *wisdom*, or its cognates, is found at least twenty-four times as Paul talked about the differences in the wisdom of this age, or the wisdom of this world, versus the wisdom of God. He said that by human wisdom, nobody can know God. God has chosen to put to flight the wisdom of the human beings in order that divine wisdom might prevail. He has chosen the foolishness of preaching to confound the wisdom of this world. So the wisdom of this age, the wisdom that is acquired by study, by discipline, or any other way, is not enough.

We need the best human wisdom that we can find. We need wisdom in government and we need wisdom in all walks of life. God gives wisdom to human beings because they are human beings. Even some atheists have ordinary wisdom, but we need more than that. Paul said, "When I come to you preaching, I choose not simply to use the tools of human wisdom. I know how to discourse. I know how to teach. I know how to use the power of persuasion through human tools. I refuse to use mere human tools in my coming to you so that your faith will not stand on human wisdom, but on divine wisdom and on the power of God."[1] Human persuasion and manipulative efforts are not sufficient to bring people to Christ. People may be able to manipulate others to the altar, but they cannot manipulate them into the kingdom of God. One must be convinced with divine wisdom about the effectiveness of the

Cross and the necessity of Jesus' death on the cross for our salvation. That is divine wisdom.

James talked about the difference between human wisdom and human shrewdness. There are a lot of shrewd people in our world who exercise their shrewdness selfishly. Two kinds of wisdom are discussed in James 3:13-18:

> Who is wise and understanding among you? Show by your good life that your works are done with gentleness born of wisdom. But if you have bitter envy and selfish ambition in your hearts, do not be boastful and false to the truth. Such wisdom does not come down from above, but is earthly, unspiritual, devilish. For where there is envy and selfish ambition, there will also be disorder and wickedness of every kind. But the wisdom from above is first pure, then peaceable, gentle, willing to yield, full of mercy and good fruits, without a trace of partiality or hypocrisy. And a harvest of righteousness is sown in peace for those who make peace.

There is a big difference between human wisdom and godly wisdom.

Every child of God, first of all, is brought into the Kingdom by becoming wise enough to know the necessity of receiving the efficacious cross of Jesus Christ, the effectiveness of His atonement. We can have wisdom available to us in our daily lives with rearing our children, being good employers or employees, or whatever the case may be. And yet, there is also the necessity in the body of Christ at critical times for a special endowment of wisdom. If we are limited to our ordinary wisdom, then we are limited in understanding how we ought to act, how we ought to live, and decisions that we ought to make. We need a special endowment of supernatural understanding which is instructive for the Body in direction, guidance, insight, and illumination. We are not dependent upon what we have acquired because God has provided the gift of wisdom.

It is likely that this gift of wisdom was operative in the apostles in Acts 6 when the problem came before them of the Grecian women who were neglected in favor of the Jewish women. Many of these apostles were businessmen. They had operated businesses with wisdom, but they also needed supernatural wisdom. The apostles considered the issue. They determined that the issue of partiality needed to be resolved. They realized, however, that their primary task was prayer and ministry of the Word. With divine wisdom, the apostles initiated a plan. To solve the pressing problem, other men were chosen to administer the daily distribution of food to the widows. The gift of wisdom is needed today in the administration of the body of Christ.

The gift of wisdom is a message of instruction. It can be short or long, but it is a message we need so that we can operate better as members of the body of Christ. Direction is needed in the body of Christ when we are baffled and do not know what to do. There are various alternate routes and only the Holy Spirit, the all-wise One, knows the route that should be chosen, and He can instruct us. Sometimes He gives us divine insight into the problem, as well as direction in solving the problem. Note again that this gift is a *message* of instruction. Not only is the speaker endowed with supernatural wisdom, but the speaker is prompted, inspired, and enabled by the Holy Spirit to *speak* the message in an understandable and meaningful way to the gathered assembly.

Very likely, the word of wisdom was operative at the Jerusalem Council. The early church had to decide what was required of individuals who were won from paganism into the Christian faith. God gave them wisdom about how to deal with the problem. He gave them insight and illumination.

The Church today needs wisdom concerning the Christian witness. How can we evangelize our community? We can formulate programs and plans, but we need the message of wisdom to direct our evangelism ministries.

Sometimes the gift of wisdom is operative without others being aware of it. Perhaps, even as the preacher is preaching the Word, or a teacher is teaching a class, there is an endowment of supernatural wisdom. This wisdom enables the preacher or teacher to speak with greater insight and illumination. Other people may think the speaker has planned these powerful words, when in actuality, the Holy Spirit provided them. The gift of wisdom enhanced the message and the fluency.

THE WORD OF KNOWLEDGE

Closely related to the word of wisdom is the word of knowledge. Some believe the major emphasis of these gifts is on "word," "message," "proclamation," "discourse," or "speech." "When the church is assembled, the Spirit bestows on some of its members the gift of instructive discourse. It is the discourse, not the wisdom or knowledge behind it, that is the spiritual gift, for it is this that is of direct service to the church."[2] In reference to the word of wisdom and the word of knowledge, Engelsen said:

> The gifts have their emphasis in the fact that they are gifts of speech, and speech prompted by the Spirit. The content is suggested by the two qualifying terms, which cover both intellectual and practical insight. By the exercise of the many and varied gifts of speech,

the worship services become both enriched
and meaningful. There is no principal difference between these two qualified terms of
speech and prophecy. They belong together
in the comprehensive category of intelligible
inspired speech. But they may well be separated, as Paul demonstrates, according to what
is mediated by them.[3]

It is true that the prompting, inspiration, and
ability to speak the message are a gift from the
Holy Spirit. What about the message itself, however? Stanley Horton said that the message is "supernatural insight into what the Bible says about
God, Christ, and God's will."[4] He continued,
"Clearly the message of knowledge has to do with
Bible truth or the application of it. It has nothing to
do with where to find lost articles or what sin or
disease a person may be suffering from—though
God can give help for these things."[5]

Is this gift a supernatural illumination of
God's Word and will? Is it a supernatural understanding of the needs of God's people? Is it a
supernatural endowment of knowledge of facts
not studied or learned? The answer is "yes" to
each of these questions. Whether knowledge
not studied, new insight into the meaning of
Scripture, and/or new insight concerning scriptural application to God's people, the message
is given as divinely inspired instruction to the
gathered assembly.

Have some considered the word of knowledge only as words spoken to individuals concerning their personal lives? God does give messages to individuals through others, but could this not also be called "revelation" or perhaps a "prophetic utterance?" Have some also shortchanged their own study of God's Word, consecration, and sensitivity to the Holy Spirit by depending on the "revelation" of others? God desires that each of us experience spiritual maturity and that we seek to be used of God to minister to the whole congregation.

Perhaps the word of knowledge was operative in the account recorded in Acts 5 in which Peter realized that Ananias had lied to the Holy Spirit, even though Ananias thought the facts were hidden.

It seems that the gift of the word of knowledge was also operative in Peter's dealings with Cornelius. After Peter's vision, he was perplexed about the meaning of it (Acts 10:17, 19). The Holy Spirit instructed him to accompany the men sent by Cornelius. Peter first shared with Cornelius and his household that God had shown him not to call any person common or unclean (v. 28). Addressing the gathered group, Peter continued, "Of a truth I perceive that God is no respecter of persons" (v. 34 KJV). The word *perceive* means to "understand." Peter addressed the Gentile group with a new knowledge that the full provisions of God were available for everybody.

Following God's outpouring of His Spirit upon Cornelius and his household, Peter shared with the Jewish brothers about God's blessings upon the Gentile believers. Peter explained how God, through a vision, had given him new knowledge of God's plan for all of His children. This message of knowledge became the basis of Peter's proclamation to the Gentile group. While Peter was preaching, God baptized the believers in the Holy Spirit. This revelation to Peter and the assembled believers has had a profound impact upon the understanding that all believers have equal access to God's grace and provision.

ENDNOTES

[1] The author's paraphrase of 1 Corinthians 2:4-5.

[2] C. K. Barrett, *A Commentary on the First Epistle to the Corinthians* (New York: Harper and Row, 1968) 284-85.

[3] Nils Ivan Johan Engelsen, *Glossalalia and the Other Forms of Inspired Speech According to I Corinthians 12-14* (Ann Arbor, MI: University Microfilms, A Xerox Company, 1971) 211.

[4] Stanley M. Horton, *I and II Corinthians* (Springfield: Logion Press, 1999) 114.

[5] *Ibid.*

STUDY GUIDE
Chapter 7

God has provided the gift of the word of wisdom and the gift of the word of knowledge to give needed instructions to the body of Christ. God views the specific needs or challenges faced by His people and supplies guidance to navigate in treacherous waters.

QUESTIONS

1. What are other terms for "word"?

2. Compare and contrast human wisdom and divine wisdom.

3. Define the word of wisdom.

4. Define the word of knowledge.

5. Reflect on these gifts in relationship to "content" and "proclamation."

8

Manifestations of Divine Power

1 Corinthians 12:8-11

THE GIFT OF FAITH

In order to be a Christian, a person must have faith. Hebrews 11:6 says, "And without faith it is impossible to please God, for whoever would approach him must believe that he exists and that he rewards those who seek him." This verse establishes the fact that faith is necessary for salvation. Ephesians 2:8-9 states, "For by grace you have been saved through faith, and this is not your own doing; it is the gift of God—not the result of works, so that no one may boast." It is not of works. It is not something that you do. Grace is a gift of God, and faith is a gift of God. Salvation is a gift of God. God enables us to exercise faith.

Faith, according to Romans 10:17, comes by hearing, and hearing by the Word of God. So the proclamation of the Word brings about, produces, or generates faith. If you want to have more faith, and if faith comes by hearing and hearing comes by the Word of God, take in the Word! Let the Word activate faith! The Scripture says, in Romans 12:3, that every believer receives a measure of faith. Note that this is talking about believers, not unbelievers. All believers are assigned a particular measure, or proportion, of faith. It is in accordance with the proportion of faith assigned that the ministries operate (v. 6).

Believers have varying degrees of faith. According to Matthew 6, Jesus talked to His disciples about not being anxious like the pagans, or not worrying like the pagans do. Further, Jesus said that if God clothes the lilies of the field, and if God gives beauty to the grass as He does, why do you not believe Him? Jesus followed this question by designating His disciples as "you of little faith" (v. 30). Persons who trust Jesus Christ for salvation but do not trust Him for daily provisions could fit in the "little faith" category.

To another person, Jesus exclaimed, "Woman, great is your faith!" (15:28). A Gentile woman came to Jesus and asked for mercy on her demon-possessed daughter. Apparently, Jesus intended His responses to challenge her to great faith. He first ignored her. His disciples tried to get Jesus to send her away. Jesus said that He was sent only to the lost sheep of the house of Israel. The woman did not retreat, but she came and worshiped Jesus and said, "Lord, help me" (v. 25). He responded, "It is not fair to take the children's food and throw it to the dogs" (v. 26). The woman said, "Yes, Lord, but even the dogs eat the crumbs that fall from their masters' table" (v. 27). She did not allow what seemed to be a put-down to deter her. In essence, she said, "Lord, You do not have to rob anybody to grant my request. It will not take a whole loaf. Just a few crumbs will meet my needs." That request prompted Jesus' reply, "Woman, great is your faith!" (v. 28).

On another occasion, a man came to Jesus and asked Him for healing for his servant. Jesus said, "I will come and heal him." The man replied, "I am not worthy for you to come under my roof. Just speak the word and he will be healed." This person understood the authority of Jesus' word. He did not have to touch the sick body, but even at a distance Jesus' spoken command would effect the healing. Jesus responded by saying, "I have not seen so great faith, no, not in Israel" (Matt. 8:10 KJV).

Even though there are different levels of faith,

the gift of faith is a divinely given endowment of extraordinary faith—the ability to believe God for supernatural intervention. This faith believes God for more than the stated promises of God. This is not pious talk that folds in a crisis. It is not empty talk or pumping someone up with psychological gimmicks, but it is laying hold on supernatural provision by divinely granted faith.

One person said the gift of faith "appears to be the God-given ability, without fakery or platitudinous exhortations, to believe what you really do not believe, to trust God for certain blessings not promised in the Scripture."[1] Another individual said the gift of faith "would seem to come upon certain of God's servants in times of special crisis or opportunity in such power that they were lifted right out of the realm of even natural and ordinary faith in God—and have a divine certainty put within their souls that triumphs over everything."[2] Yet another said, "It probably refers to a supernatural conviction that God will reveal his power or mercy in a special way in a specific instance."[3]

Perhaps the gift of faith was operative in Paul during the storm. The wind still raged, the waves pounded against the ship, the rain still fell in torrents. Paul stood in the darkness of the hour and proclaimed, "I believe God to spare all the occupants of the ship" (see Acts 27:22-25).

Sometimes the Church faces a crisis. God can endow a believer with the gift of faith that will see results. A state of desperation can be changed into hopefulness within the people of God because of the gift of faith.

THE GIFTS OF HEALINGS

God placed within the natural body certain healing processes. God also gave knowledge to the medical profession so that they can sometimes block the hindrances and enhance our healing possibilities. The gifts of healings are not referring to the natural processes or the medical profession, however. The gifts of healings are supernatural endowments that bring cures for all kinds of sicknesses and diseases.

God desires that a healing atmosphere prevail in the body of believers. This is an atmosphere of trust, expectation, and mutual consideration. In this atmosphere, there is a strong belief in the mighty power of God, a strong belief in the effectiveness of prayer, and believers take seriously the exhortation found in James 5:13-16:

> Are any among you suffering? They should pray. Are any cheerful? They should sing songs of praise. Are any among you sick? They should call for the elders of the church and have them pray over them, anointing them with oil in the name of the Lord. The prayer of faith will save the sick, and the Lord will raise them up; and anyone who has committed

sins will be forgiven. Therefore confess your
sins to one another, and pray for one another,
so that you may be healed. The prayer of the
righteous is powerful and effective.

The sick demonstrate their faith by summon-
ing the elders of the church. The elders believe
and pray for healing. The atmosphere of trust
should prevail so that if the sick have sinned,
their sins can be confessed. The believers are
exhorted to pray for one another so that healings will occur. The "prayer of faith" that brings
healing can be separate from or associated with
the gift of faith and/or the gifts of healings.

For the first time in the listing of the gifts in 1
Corinthians 12:8-10, the plural words are used—
gifts of healings.[4] Various possible reasons for the
plurals are offered. (1) There are many different
diseases that require many divine cures. Grosheide said, "The plural 'gifts' may indicate healings of various illnesses. Each illness requires a
special charisma."[5] (2) God endows different
people through whom the gifts of healings are
operative. Some even seem to be used of God to
minister to certain types of illnesses. The term
gifts of healings "strongly suggests that there were
different gifts of healings: not everyone was getting healed by one person, and perhaps certain
persons with *one* of these gifts of healing could
by God's grace heal certain diseases or heal a

variety of diseases but only at certain times." (3) Each illness to be healed takes a new and special supernatural endowment. "The plural *charismata* probably suggests not a permanent gift, as it were, but that each occurrence is a 'gift' in its own right."[7] Bittlinger said, "Every healing is a special gift. In this way the spiritually gifted individual stands always in new dependence upon the Divine Giver."[8]

For every sickness or disease, God can provide the gift of healing that is necessary through any Spirit-filled believer. This gift may operate regularly in that person's life, occasionally, or as a onetime manifestation. The gift is not operated by human desire or human will, but by the Sovereign Lord.

As believers we need to consecrate ourselves, practice obedience, pray in faith, and expect God to heal individuals. God alone, however, determines whether, how, and when healing takes place.

WORKINGS OF MIRACLES

This gift could also be called "workings of powers." The plural terms in this gift could reflect the multiplicity of powers manifested, as well as the different persons through whom they are manifested. These workings of miracles are extraordinary manifestations of supernatural power.

At certain times, God chooses to reveal His power. In the Exodus account, God showed that His power superseded political power, psychic powers, and all other earthly powers. He showed His power over nature itself.

Jesus' ministry was characterized by preaching, teaching, and miracles. These miracles include healings, exorcisms, and demonstrations of power over the natural order. In the Gospel of Mark, the word translated "miracle" is the same word used in this gift, a "work of power."[9] In the Gospel of John the word translated "miracle" means a "sign."[10] It is a sign-miracle, a miracle that points beyond itself to deity. The miracle of Jesus' multiplying the bread and fish points to the fact that Jesus alone is the Bread of Life. Jesus' raising of Lazarus from the dead substantiated His claim, "I am the resurrection; and the life" (John 11:25). The principle established is that miracles meet human needs and glorify God. The gift of the workings of miracles should do no less.

Several instances of the workings of miracles were evident in the early church. Dorcas was dead and she was brought back to life (Acts 9:40). Eutychus was dead and he was brought back to life (20:10). "Extraordinary miracles" occurred involving handkerchiefs and aprons that had touched Paul's body. Sicknesses were cured

and evil spirits departed when these handkerchiefs were laid on others (19:11-12).

Since there are no gifts labeled "gifts of exorcism," it seems that the gifts of the workings of
miracles are operative in the casting out of de-
mons. The exorcism is a manifestation of the su-
periority of divine power over evil powers. The
exorcism meets a human need for freedom and
glorifies God.

Certainly there are areas of interrelatedness
among the manifestations of power. A miraculous healing, for example, could be a manifestation of the gifts of healings, the workings of
miracles, or even the gift of faith. The workings
of miracles would include, however, works of
power not related to physical healings.

ENDNOTES

[1] D. A. Carson, *Showing the Spirit* (Grand Rapids: Baker Books, 1987) 39.

[2] Donald Gee, *Concerning Spiritual Gifts* (Springfield: Gospel Publishing House, 1947) 36.

[3] Gordon Fee, *The First Epistle of the Corinthians*, 593.

[4] Other plurals in the list are workings of miracles, discernments of spirits, and kinds of tongues.

[5] F. W. Grosheide, *Commentary of the First Epistle to the Corinthians* (Grand Rapids: William B. Eerdmans, 1953) 286.

[6] D. A. Carson, *Showing the Spirit*, 39.

[7] Gordon Fee, *The First Epistle to the Corinthians*, 594.

[8] Arnold Bittlinger. *Gifts and Graces*, trans. Herbert Klassen (Grand Rapids: William B. Eerdmans, 1967) 37.

[9] The Greek word is *dunamis*.

[10] The Greek word is *semeion*.

STUDY GUIDE
Chapter 8

The gift of faith, the gifts of healings, and the workings of miracles are manifestations of divine power. The Holy Spirit distributes these gifts to meet needs and challenges of the people of God. Reflect on their similarities and differences.

QUESTIONS

1. How is the gift of faith distinguished from the faith necessary for salvation and for living the Christian life?

2. What is the relationship between the prayer of faith that results in healing and the gifts of healings?

3. List two possible reasons for the plurals in *gifts of healings*.

4. How would you define the workings of miracles?

5. List three examples of workings of miracles.

9

Gifts of Exposition and Discernment

THE GIFT OF PROPHECY

We are familiar with the Old Testament prophet. The most prominent term translated "prophet" means "to flow forth." This term emphasizes the Word of God that is spoken forth from the prophet. Another word that is rarely used is the word meaning "seer." The prophet was called a "seer" because he was given special insight from God. The prophet received a message from God and spoke that message from God.

The prophet's major task was to warn God's people of the consequences of disobedience to God and to call them to full compliance to God's will. The prophet's message sometimes had a predictive element, especially enlightening God's people of God's future action. The prophet also sometimes pronounced judgment upon the enemies of God.

Not everybody was called to be a prophet. Moses wished, however, that all God's children would be prophets (Num. 11:29). Joel anticipated the day when God would pour out His Spirit and sons and daughters would prophesy (Joel 2:28-32). Peter said that Joel's prophecy began to be fulfilled on the day of Pentecost when the disciples were baptized in the Holy Spirit (Acts 2:16-21). Today, the gift of prophecy can be operative in any child of God. Paul said, "Do not despise prophesying, but test everything; and hold fast what is good" (1 Thess. 5:20-21 RSV). These reminders need to be heard and heeded today when skepticism and cynicism abound. Building a high trust level in the congregation and knowing those who labor among us increase the possibilities of giving and/or receiving prophecies.

The gift of prophecy is a message from God given spontaneously in the language understood by the people. Its primary purposes are to edify, to encourage, and/or to comfort. The gift of prophecy is a "sign" to the believers (1 Cor. 14:22). The word *sign* could be translated "sign-miracle." It is a miracle that points beyond itself. The gift of prophecy is a miraculous intervention of God as He gives a message to His people. This miracle testifies to the manifest-presence of God among His people. It glorifies God as the all-wise God who knows His own intimately and cares enough to give them a specific message to meet their needs. Arrington states:

> The gift of prophecy functions as an edifying gift. It assures God's people that He knows them intimately and is aware of the dangers they are facing. He has them in His hand, leading and encouraging them. Paul, therefore, states that the purpose of prophecy is that everyone may learn and be encouraged (1 Cor. 14:31).[1]

The gift of prophecy is not a prepared sermon or lesson. However, while a person is preaching or teaching, the gift of prophecy can become operative. This prophetic utterance can be by the preacher or teacher, or by someone else in the congregation. The message is from God, the inspiration is from God, and the speaking forth is guided by God.

In addition to edifying, encouraging, or comforting believers, the gift of prophecy can have profound effects upon unbelievers. The gift of prophecy can convict of sin, call persons into account for the way they are living, and/or reveal the secrets of a person's heart (v. 25).

THE GIFT OF DISCERNMENTS OF SPIRITS

Hundreds were gathered for the closing session of a training conference. Except for the keynote speaker, the participants were seated on the stage. When the keynote speaker walked across the stage and sat down beside the moderator, he immediately asked the moderator, "Who is that man on the third seat from you?" The moderator explained that the man was scheduled to give a testimony of an occurrence in Vietnam. The speaker said, "Something is wrong. Please don't allow him to speak today." In spite of the warning, the man was allowed to speak. His speech was passionate and persuasive. Because of the warning, however, the person was investigated and found to be a fraud. He had never even served in Vietnam. The gift of discernments of spirits was operative, but unfortunately not heeded quickly enough. Many people who heard the speech became confused when they later heard about the fraudulent nature of the speech. Some of them asked themselves, "How could I have been swayed by him?"

In order to understand and appreciate the gift of discernments better, let us discuss biblical discernment. The root word is *judge*. The meaning of *judge* is determined primarily by its context. The word is used to refer to a person who assumes the place of the final judge. God alone is the final judge. No human being should be as presumptuous as to attempt to stand in God's place. Judging also refers to a "judgmental" attitude, which is a supercritical attitude. As part of His Sermon on the Mount in Matthew 7:1-5, Jesus condemned this kind of attitude. A positive use of "judging" is distinguishing, discerning, or making discriminating choices. According to the writer of Hebrews, one mark of spiritual maturity is the ability to distinguish (judge) good from evil. "But solid food is for the mature, for those whose faculties have been trained by practice to distinguish good from evil" (5:14). Every Christian should cultivate the development of discernment. Proper discernment will keep a Christian from the extremes of cynicism or gullibility.

The need for spiritual discernment is great. Jesus warned, "Beware of false prophets, who come to you in sheep's clothing but inwardly are ravenous wolves" (Matt. 7:15). This discerning is helped by knowing the character of the ones who claim to be prophets. Jesus further said that the last days will be characterized by the multiplying of false prophets who will lead many astray (24:11, 24).

To encourage discernment, the apostle John used a different word than the one we have been examining. This word emphasizes "putting to the test in order to prove." "Beloved, do not believe every spirit, but test the spirits to see whether they are from God; for many false prophets have gone out into the world" (1 John 4:1). Paul used this same word when he said, "Do not despise prophesying, but test everything; hold fast what is good" (1 Thess. 5:20-21 RSV). These exhortations underscore the urgent need for spiritual discernment.

In addition to our ability to discern, honed by knowledge of God's Word and a growing sensitivity to the Holy Spirit, God has provided the gift of discernments of spirits for the gathered assembly. This gift is a supernatural endowment to distinguish, or discern, the spirit with which something is said or done. The plurals, *discernments of spirits*, indicate different kinds of discerning of different spirits. Therefore, the question needs to be considered, "Is this from the Holy Spirit, from evil spirits, or from the human spirit?" Paul warned that there are persons preaching a different Jesus, a different spirit, and a different gospel. These persons claim to be super-apostles. However, they are "false apostles, deceitful workers, disguising themselves as apostles of Christ. And no wonder! Even Satan disguises himself as an angel of light. So it is not strange if his ministers also disguise themselves as ministers of righteousness. Their end will match their deeds" (2 Cor. 11:13-15). With charm, enticing words, lying wonders, and exalted claims of super-spirituality, Satan's emissaries are deceiving many people. We need the Holy Spirit's gift of discernments of spirits to rescue us from these schemes.

The human spirit is also capable of producing spiritual substitutes. Many of these are hidden in spiritual language and personal hype. Sometimes it is impossible to recognize the fallacy of these substitutes without the supernatural endowment of discernment. Sometimes, actions that seem to be right flow from wrong motives.

Given the deceitfulness of evil spirits and of the human spirit, many just give up on spiritual manifestations. There are genuine manifestations, however, because the Holy Spirit is at work among the people of God. His work is trustworthy, and His work stands the test of judging, proving, or discerning. The gift of discernments of spirits gives us confidence and freedom in the work of God.

The gift of discernments of spirits seems closely related to the gift of prophecy. Paul gave instruction that others should judge, or discern, the prophetic utterances (1 Cor. 14:29-30). Paul's exhortation that we noted earlier said, "Do not despise prophesying, but test everything" (1 Thess. 5:20-21 RSV). The gift of discernments of spirits does not foster an atmosphere of resistance or distrust, but an atmosphere of acceptance of God's work and a confidence of divine confirmation. The

Holy Spirit will not allow us to be led astray by any words or any actions at any point, because He will give discernment.

Let us consider some possible origins of a prophetic utterance.

1. It may be precisely God's message.

2. It may be an evil spirit's message.

3. It may be the message of a human being who desires a certain thing for the recipient.

4. It may be that God gave a message to a person and he/she then added his/her own interpretation or human desires to the message.[2]

These possibilities should help us realize the urgency of spiritual discernment. These possibilities should help us to appreciate the gift of discernments of spirits and to listen carefully to God's direction through its exercise.

ENDNOTES

[1] French L. Arrington, *Encountering the Holy Spirit* (Cleveland, TN: Pathway Press, 2003) 336.

[2] John A. Lombard Jr., *Introduction to Christian Ministries II* (Cleveland, TN: External Studies Program, Lee College, 1993) 82.

STUDY GUIDE
Chapter 9

The gift of prophecy is supplied by the Holy Spirit for the Church to be edified, encouraged, and comforted. The message is directed by God and given in the language of the people. The gift of discernments of spirits is needed when the gift of prophecy is operated, as well as at other times in the life of the Church.

QUESTIONS

1. In what way can the gift of prophecy be called a gift of exposition?

2. What are the primary purposes of the gift of prophecy?

3. What are the results of the gift of prophecy in relationship to unbelievers?

4. How would you define the gift of discernments of spirits?

5. What are different meanings of the word *judge*?

6. What is the primary indicator of which meaning the word *judge* has?

7. Memorize 1 Thessalonians 5:20-21.

10

The Twin Gifts of Intelligible Speech

THE GIFT OF VARIOUS KINDS OF TONGUES

If someone speaks several languages, does that mean that the person has the gift of tongues? This individual does have a special ability to *learn* languages. However, when speaking in tongues is discussed in the New Testament, the languages are neither studied nor learned, but they are given by the Holy Spirit. The Holy Spirit inspires the language and provides the syllables that make up the language. The speaker cooperates with the Holy Spirit and speaks what the Spirit provides. The speaker is not taken over by the Spirit nor coerced by the Spirit.

Speaking in other tongues as the initial evidence of the baptism in the Holy Spirit and the continuing ministry of speaking in tongues in one's private devotional life are differentiated in function from the gift of tongues listed in 1 Corinthians 12:10. The primary difference is edifying the individual versus edifying the body of believers. We will discuss this difference more fully in the section "Guidelines."

Some persons raise questions about the nature of "tongues." Are they human languages or heavenly languages?

> Some of these were speaking known languages, because many who were in Jerusalem for the Feast of Pentecost heard them speaking in their own dialects. Many of the listeners were devout individuals, and they were amazed as they heard and understood these Galileans speak forth the mighty works of God. Curious, they were asking one another, "What does this mean?" Others had a totally different response. They said, "They are filled with new wine" (Acts 2:12-13). We do not know what aroused this skepticism and hostility. Perhaps some heard speech that was not a known language.[1]

Paul used the term "various kinds of tongues" (1 Cor. 12:10). Some manifestations of tongues could be human languages and some known only to God. The Holy Spirit is all-wise and is in charge of which kind of tongues to manifest at each occasion. Dr. Arrington says that "tongues are languages given by the Holy Spirit and may be either human or angelic. If the language is an earthly one, usually individuals listening to the gifted person do not understand what is being said. However, sometimes individuals who speak a different language than the speaker may hear their own native tongue."[2]

Speaking in tongues is a unique reciprocity between God and the believer in which the Holy Spirit is giving the utterance and simultaneously the believer is speaking it. The utterance may be directed to God as praises or cries of inarticulate groanings (Rom. 8:26) and the speaker is being built up. On the other hand, in the gathered assembly, the utterance is meant to be interpreted so that the body of Christ may be built up.

Along with the ministry to believers, the gift of tongues serves as "a sign . . . for unbelievers" (1 Cor. 14:22). As God got the attention of the resistant and spoke judgment to them through foreign tongues, so He gets the attention of unbelievers through the gift of tongues. When these tongues are interpreted, many of these unbelievers are convicted and judged, and the secrets of their hearts are revealed. Many fall on their faces in worship to God and declare that God is really among you (vv. 20-25).

THE GIFT OF INTERPRETATION
OF TONGUES

I have referred to the gift of tongues and the gift of the interpretation of tongues as "twin gifts for intelligible speech" because God's message is communicated to the gathered body by their working together. In the operation of the gift of interpretation of tongues, the Holy Spirit prompts a believer to give the meaning of what has been spoken in another language. The "meaning" is not necessarily a translation, but the "interpretation" of the message in tongues. The Holy Spirit provides to the interpreter the meaning of what was spoken in tongues. The interpreter could be one ordinarily used by God for this ministry, the one who spoke the message in other tongues, or any other believer chosen by the Holy Spirit.

The gift of interpretation completes the process of communication begun in the gift of tongues. The message is now intelligible to the gathered congregation.

GUIDELINES FOR
THE GIFT OF TONGUES,
THE GIFT OF INTERPRETATION,
AND THE GIFT OF PROPHECY
1 Corinthians 14

Love should undergird and motivate every ministry, every operation, and every gift in the

Church. When believers are gathered for worship, each should be intent on the edifying of the whole body. Love precludes self-interest, self-promotion, and self-satisfaction. Each believer should be eager for mutual upbuilding to take place in the body of Christ.

In giving guidelines for the gift of tongues, the gift of interpretation, and the gift of prophecy in the gathered assembly, Paul instructed the congregation so that the purposes of these gifts would be fully realized. Paul did not disparage either gift, nor did he prohibit either gift. He identified the purposes of each and the appropriate operation in corporate worship. Paul revealed some of the blessings of prophecy to edify the body and some of the blessings of speaking in tongues to edify the individual believer.

The believer is encouraged to pursue love and to seek spiritual gifts, especially prophecy. The gift of prophecy is speaking to the people in language they understand. It speaks to upbuild, encourage, and comfort. For the purpose of edifying the body of Christ, the one who prophesies is greater than the one who speaks in tongues *unless* someone interprets the message. Neither gift is intrinsically a better gift or a lesser gift. The greater gift is the one that fulfills the need at hand. In the instance of the gathered assembly, the need is for the whole body to be edified.

That need is fulfilled by a message understood by the people, whether it be the gift of prophecy or the gift of tongues accompanied by the gift of interpretation. The believer is urged to seek to excel in building up the Church.

The person speaking in tongues is speaking to God rather than to others. Others do not understand, but the person is speaking mysteries in the Spirit. The speaker in tongues is being built up, but unless the message is interpreted, the congregation is not built up. The one speaking in tongues gives thanks well, but the uninstructed cannot say "Amen" because of not understanding what is being said. The person who speaks out in tongues in the gathered assembly should pray for an interpretation in order that the body be edified. If the speaker does not receive the interpretation and no one else interprets the message, then the person should be silent in the church and speak to himself and to God. In this arrangement the flow of the worship is not disrupted, but the speaker is edified. When the message in tongues is interpreted, as in prophecy, the church is built up, encouraged, and comforted. The unbeliever is convinced of the presence of God and convicted of sin.

While Paul gave definite guidelines for the gift of tongues, he personally encouraged speaking in tongues. He said, "Now I would like all of you to speak in tongues, but even more to prophesy" (1 Cor. 14:5). Paul said that when he prayed in a tongue, his mind was unproductive, but that he would pray and sing with the Spirit and that he would pray and sing with his mind also (vv. 14-15). Paul also said, "I thank God that I speak in tongues more than all of you; nevertheless, in church I would rather speak five words with my mind, in order to instruct others also, than ten thousand words in a tongue" (vv. 18-19). He concluded by saying, "Be eager to prophesy, and do not forbid speaking in tongues" (v. 39).

Paul also gave guidelines for the gift of prophecy. The ones prophesying should prophesy one by one so that all may learn and be encouraged and that order and peace may prevail. If another receives a revelation, the one speaking should be silent. The church is to weigh carefully, or discern, what has been spoken by each person who prophesies.

ENDNOTES

[1] John A. Lombard Jr. and Jerald J. Daffe, *Speaking in Tongues: Initial Evidence of Spirit Baptism?* (Cleveland, TN: Pathway Press, 2005) 79-80.

[2] French L. Arrington, *Encountering the Holy Spirit* (Cleveland, TN: Pathway Press, 2003) 341.

STUDY GUIDE
Chapter 10

The gift of tongues probably causes more discussion than any other gift. This gift plus the gift of interpretation of tongues fulfills a similar function as the gift of prophecy. The function of speaking in tongues in private devotions differs from speaking in tongues in the gathered assembly. The guidelines in 1 Corinthians 14 give freedom and structure in the operation of these two gifts and the gift of prophecy.

QUESTIONS

1. How do you differentiate speaking in tongues as initial evidence of Holy Spirit baptism, His continuing ministry, and the speaking in tongues in the gathered assembly?

2. Why are the gift of tongues and the gift of interpretation of tongues called "the twin gifts of intelligible speech"?

3. What are some possible differences between translation and interpretation?

4. Discuss the guidelines in 1 Corinthians 14.

11

Gifts to Benefit All

1 Corinthians 12:28-30
Romans 12:1-8

When you think of spiritual gifts, do you ordinarily think of the nine gifts listed in 1 Corinthians 12:8-10? How many of the other gifts could you recall without checking the passages in Romans 12:6-8 and 1 Corinthians 12:28? Some of the gifts listed in these passages overlap ones that we have already discussed. The emphasis in each location is on the diversity of gifts that God has provided for the Church.

1 Corinthians 12:28-30

After using the analogy of the body to the church and its members, Paul said that God has appointed in the Church, first, apostles; second, prophets; and, third, teachers. God is responsible for the diversity in the body of Christ. The order of these first three ministries most likely simply indicates their foundational nature in the early church. We discussed these gifts to the Body in our discussion of Ephesians 4:11-16.

Paul included in this list of gifts, miracles, gifts of healings, and various kinds of tongues. These were explored in the discussion of 1 Corinthians 12:8-10.

Paul introduced two gifts that have not been discussed earlier. The first is the gift of helps. The plural word could indicate various kinds of helps. It could be translated "helpful deeds."[1] Although all believers should be involved in helping others, some Christians are enabled by the Holy Spirit to offer special help to others. These helps take various forms, such as helping the weak, providing for the poor, or giving special assistance to members of the body of Christ. These helps may seem so "ordinary" that some may not attribute them to a spiritual gift. The gift may become apparent in the extraordinary number of ordinary helps that a person performs.

The second of these gifts listed in 1 Corinthians 12:28 is the gift of governings, which is sometimes translated "administrations." The word is used in Acts 27:11 as a pilot or helmsman of a ship. "It implies guidance and counseling, or even the managing of business affairs as well as

giving spiritual leadership to the local assembly."[2]
This spiritual gift enables the recipient to give enhanced spiritual guidance to God's people.

At the end of this list, Paul asked a series of
rhetorical questions with the expected answer
to be "No." The question essentially was "Does
everyone operate in every one of these gifts in
the gathered assembly?" Some emphasize the
question "Do all speak with tongues?" because it
seems to support their contention that not every
Spirit-baptized believer will speak in tongues.
This question is posed, however, to refer to the
gift of tongues manifested in the public assembly with the intention that the gift of interpretation will follow so that the message will be understood. This question deals *only* with the gift
of tongues in the gathered body and not with
the initial evidence or the ongoing ministry of
tongues in the life of the believer.

Romans 12:1-8

Paul urged believers to make a full commitment of themselves to God in order to be transformed and enabled to live out the Christian life
in this world. He urged believers to sober thinking, a thinking that acknowledges that each is
only a part of the Body, but that each is intricate-
ly related to the other parts. With sober thinking, each can operate fully in the gift assigned

and not attempt to do more. The gifts assigned are by the Sovereign Lord and according to the measure of faith assigned.

Since we discussed the gift of prophecy and the gift of teaching earlier, let us note the other gifts listed in this passage. Paul said that if you have the gift of service, then fulfill it by serving. The service could involve many things, such as preparing meals for the sick, assisting the poor or disabled, or servicing the car of a single parent. Even though these tasks are sometimes done by unbelievers, believers provide these as spiritual services, done as unto the Lord. The gift of service increases the frequency and the intensity of this ministry of assisting others.

The gift of exhortation is mentioned next. The word *exhortation* means "encouragement," "consolation," or "comfort." The gift of exhortation enables a person to offer special encouragement to individuals experiencing affliction and to offer comfort to those experiencing grief. "Exhortation needs to be directed to the cultivation of patience and perseverance and these are closely related to consolation."[3]

Even though all Christians should give of their possessions, some are endowed with the gift of giving. This giving should be done with single-mindedness or purity of motive.

> Giving must not be done with the ulterior mo-
> tives of securing influence and advantage for
> oneself, a vice too frequently indulged by the
> affluent in their donations to the treasury of
> the church and to which these responsible for
> the direction of the affairs of the church are too
> liable to succumb.[4]

The word translated "single-mindedness" or "simplicity" could also be translated "generosity" or "liberality." Single-mindedness seems to be the most appropriate.

The person exercising the gift of leadership should do so with diligence. Some translations say, "he who leads," and some say, "he who gives aid." Each is a viable possibility because the word means both things. The verb form was used by Paul in 1 Thessalonians 5:12 and 1 Timothy 3:4. "The primary meaning is 'to lead, govern.' The idea of 'going before' evolved into the notion of 'to protect, care' . . . those who would lead in the church must do so by caring and serving."[5]

Dr. Arrington commented, "The word *proiste-mi* was not only used to describe leadership, but a second meaning was 'to care for' or 'to give aid.' It is not necessary to choose one meaning and exclude the other. The two meanings are not mutually exclusive."[6] Spiritual leadership involves caring for those who are being lead. The word *diligence* can mean "earnest care."[7]

This word underscores the way spiritual leadership should be carried out.

The gift of showing mercy is the last one in the list in Romans. *"Eleos* is a broad term that sometimes has the sense of sympathy or pity. The term is used to describe the act of the Samaritan in the familiar parable (Luke 10:37)."[8] This parable of Jesus shows us that mercy flowed out of compassion in a practical act of kindness that could not be demanded by the recipient. The gift of mercy is energized by the Holy Spirit to help individuals in need. Whatever help is given should be with cheerfulness. The word translated "cheerfulness" is the word from which we get our English word *hilarity*. Showing mercy should not be done morosely or grudgingly, but with a lively and buoyant attitude and approach.

ENDNOTES

[1] Gordon D. Fee, *The First Epistle to the Corinthians* (Grand Rapids: William B. Eerdmans Publishing Company, 1987) 621.

[2] Stanley M. Horton, *I & II Corinthians* (Springfield: Logion Press, 1999) 123.

[3] John Murray, *The Epistle to the Romans (Vol. 2)* (Grand Rapids: William B. Eerdmans Publishing Company, 1968) 125.

[4] Murray, *op. cit.*, 126.

[5] William D. Mounce, *Word Biblical Commentary, Vol. 46, Pastoral Epistles* (Nashville: Thomas Nelson Publishers, 2000) 178.

[6] French L. Arrington, *Encountering the Holy Spirit* (Cleveland, TN: Pathway Press, 2003) 300.

[7] Marvin R. Vincent, *Word Studies in the New Testament* (Wilmington, DE: Associated Publishers and Authors, 1972) 743.

[8] Anthony D. Palma, *The Holy Spirit: A Pentecostal Perspective* (Springfield: Logion Press, 2001) 219.

STUDY GUIDE
Chapter 11

God is the Author of diversity in the body of Christ. This diversity operates to create and maintain unity. Each gift is an intricate part of the Body. Each function is a unique and necessary part of the health of the Body.

QUESTIONS

1. How does God compare the human body and the spiritual Body?

2. Compare and contrast the gift of helps and the gift of service.

3. Compare and contrast the gift of governings and the gift of leading.

4. Reflect upon the attitude with which each gift is to be carried out.

12

Common Misconceptions

These were the words of a sincere believer who appeared to want to be of service in the Kingdom: "I am praying to receive all the gifts of the Spirit." His desire for spiritual giftedness was excellent. But, assuredly, there was a combination of ignorance and misconception.

It seems similar to the time when the mother of James and John came to Jesus with her sons and asked for each of them to be seated in places of honor in His kingdom.[1] He responded first to her saying, "You don't know what you are asking." Then he turned to the two men and asked, "Can you drink the cup I am going to drink?" They affirmed by saying, "We can."

More than likely these two disciples, members of Jesus' inner circle of three, were sincere in their desires. They apparently felt secure in their abilities and view of the future.

It's definitely questionable if they had much of a grasp of the cost they would pay to fulfill their ministry.

Misconceptions can lead to costly errors of judgment as well as becoming immersed in both doctrinal and practical errors. Consider the difficulties which may appear or hinder the life of the person who made the opening statement.

1. Because of the emphasis on number, it becomes easy to allow a competitiveness of extraspirituality to replace the desire for ministry.

2. Desiring all of the gifts completely destroys the concept of each member of the Church body being a necessary contributing member.

3. Closely related to the previous difficulty is the possibility of discouraging others in the Body from either seeking or further developing their spiritual gift.

How do these various misconceptions come into existence? Of course, the basic reason is biblical ignorance. Mentioned in a previous chapter, but bearing repeating, is the apostle Paul's statement to the Corinthian believers: "Now about spiritual gifts, brothers, I do not want you to be ignorant" (1 Cor. 12:1). Ignorance spawns unusual ideas from some individuals when allowed to speak from the reservoir of "I think" or "I feel." Sadly some of them may rise from their belief of the Spirit's impressing these ideas on their heart and mind.

A second reason for misconceptions in spiritual matters stems from a previous environment. In verse 2, Paul pointed to the Corinthians past life of being pagans and its impacting influence. A previous environment may be the principles followed in our pre-Christian life or the guiding principles of our educational pursuits. Not to be overlooked are mentors and other major influences—a parent, other family member, employer, or pastor. Many of them are extremely positive but, when it comes to spiritual gifts, may foster erroneous conceptions.

Then there is a third reason which needs our consideration. It is the minimum amount of specific instruction concerning spiritual gifts contained within Scripture. Most of us probably wish the Lord had provided an extended glossary of terms and an extended list of instructions. However, in the absence of both it becomes easy to make assumptions. This may be the result of limited experience or being influenced by someone who also is ignorant but creating their own concepts.

The remainder of this chapter will consider nine misconceptions. You will notice several of them touch on ideas that received consideration

in previous chapters. Some duplication is necessary in order to provide the emphasis necessary
on each topic. Also, the order of presentation of
these misconceptions should not be interpreted
as signifying the frequency of their appearing
within the body of believers.

MISCONCEPTION # 1
GIFTS ARE SIGN OF
SPIRITUAL MATURITY

If this were true, local churches would not be
torn apart at worst or rendered ineffective at
best by petty issues! If this were true, we would
not see leaders falling into scandalous situations
that bring shame and reproach on the body of
Christ! If this were true, individual believers
would continually be seeking for the good of the
whole Body rather than pursuing self-interest!

Spiritual maturity is a process of discipleship. If
we were forced to wait until a certain level of spiritual maturity were attained until spiritual giftedness were to appear in believers' lives, this would
result in a limitation of the Spirit's work both in
the Church and the surrounding areas. Consider
this example: A young man is gifted in evangelism. When witnessing he speaks with ease. But,
in normal conversation he stutters and struggles
with communication. Fearlessly, he approaches
exceptionally "rough-looking characters," shares
Christ, and they listen!

Who knows how many people would never hear the message of Christ if this giftedness were withheld until this young man reached a certain level of "spirituality."

Tied closely to this misconception of spiritual maturity is the idea of being "perfect" or never sinning. Regretfully, but true, the reality of our being in fleshly bodies living in a sinful world negatively impacts us. Sometimes temptation drives us to an attitude or action for which we need to repent. There are occasions when we struggle with certain sins and are in the process of sanctification. God doesn't automatically "shut off" our giftedness. They are gifts of God's grace, not gifts of our perfection.

The church at Corinth provides an excellent example. The Holy Spirit was active in this church. But as might be expected there were some definite signs of immaturity. By God's grace they had been plucked out of sin and transformed into followers of Christ. But, there were some intense struggles that had to be overcome. The apostle Paul even addressed them as not only being babes in Christ but also described them as being carnal or worldly (1 Cor. 3:1). They were guilty of jealousy, quarreling, arrogance, and even immorality. Having said all this, it does not mean individuals can continue for an extended period in their sins and still operate in their giftedness.

Samson provides us with an excellent example. The miraculous birth preceded by the angel's message of his being a deliverer of Israel sets the stage for the Holy Spirit's using him through feats of strength. Even after an immoral liaison with a prostitute he ripped up the doors and posts of Gaza and carried them miles from the city (Judg. 16:1-3). He flirted with disaster as Delilah begged to know the secret of his strength. Finally, he crossed the line but didn't realize it. One of the saddest scenes in Scripture is Samson's awakening, assuming he would go out as other times, unaware of the Lord's leaving him (v. 20).

This same scenario may apply to the person who assumes their spiritual giftedness will continue despite unconfessed sin and failing to fight temptation. Regretfully, we have seen too many of these situations in recent decades. Individuals with national ministries were found to be involved in adulterous relationships, spousal abuse, closet homosexuality, pornography addiction, and financial mismanagement. Yet, for a period of time, their ministry was blessing people. These same situations are known to occur on a local-church level. However, eventually sins are exposed and God chooses to stop ministry through them.

Maybe there is an occasion when you question why God is using a person whose failings are known to you. God's grace and desire for the body to receive this ministry even from an imperfect vessel who is growing in faith may be one reason. Not to be overlooked is the possibility of others not submitting to the work of the Holy Spirit so the Body may be edified.

MISCONCEPTION # 2
GIFTS ARE MINISTRY
WITH NO PRICE TO PAY

> Is there a price to pay for the gifts? If there were, they would not be gifts, but purchases. Nevertheless, there may well be a price to pay in their use, to serve God with them. Those not prepared to risk their leisure, comfort, reputation and perhaps much more may be little used by God—even if He does bestow His powerful gifts upon them.[2]

As seen in previous chapters, some gifts are very upfront or public in their operation. Others are behind the scenes and rarely known to many. Regardless of the giftedness or setting, there may be a price to pay for the honor of being used by the Holy Spirit in ministering to others. This reality may slide by many of us who live in a comfortable setting in which spiritual activities are considered normal. Yet, even then, there are those who may have difficulty with the operation of the spiritual gifts.

The price to pay may vary from person to person and the giftedness which is operating. Vulnerability is one aspect. This is especially true of the more public gifts. Individuals become vulnerable to misunderstanding and even accusations by those who do not understand the gift or assume it should be offered only in private. Not to be overlooked is jealousy that may occur within those who wish they were in the public eye.

The price to pay may be continued unwarranted criticism. For example, "If they really had the gift of healing, then more people would be healed!" This is totally unfair, since we know there are many other factors that are a part of each situation other than the ministering person. Criticism may be leveled at one's personal life simply due to not following their life patterns. Some individuals assume there is only one way to live, and it is the one they have adopted. It has nothing to do with biblical guidelines of holiness. A statement from past decades summarizes this: "If you wear one feather in your hat, it isn't enough. But if you wear two feathers, it is too many!"

The price to pay may be in the amount of physical effort and time necessary to minister within one's gift. The gifts of helps and administration may take hours from one's free time. These often are behind-the-scenes activities that go unnoticed except when not fulfilled and go unrecognized for the amount of effort to accomplish the task.

For some, this price to pay means stepping outside of one's normal comfort zone to be effective. This may mean becoming more aggressive in words and actions when your natural tendency is to be rather quiet and in the shadows. Not to be overlooked may be the necessity of the outgoing person learning to patiently wait for the right moment or opportunity to be the most effective.

We would do a grave injustice not to include the growing of one's life as a price to pay. Some individuals are called to exercise not only their faith in Christ but their spiritual gifts in a hostile environment. Believers, who are citizens of countries unfavorable to Christianity, as well as missionaries, may pay this supreme price.

MISCONCEPTION # 3
GIFTS CONFIRM A PERSON'S METHODOLOGY

Have you ever heard someone say, "I'm not responsible for what I do or say when moving under the anointing of the Holy Spirit"? The sad part of this is the statement tends to go unchallenged. Associated with this are the many accounts of individuals breaking glasses or crutches prior to praying for a person's healing. In His sovereignty God chooses not to heal those particular people even though many others have been with the same circumstances. One question stands out: Who pays to replace those glasses or crutches?

Techniques and procedures never are validated by the end result. Our personal formulas that may be beneficial in ministry must not to be seen as the right way simply because the Body is edified as a whole and individual's lives are changed and prayers answered. At times, God may be gracious and work through us when the methodology isn't correct because of wanting to benefit His people.

Some years ago, the late Dr. Robert Webber shared a pattern from the early church that we have adopted when praying for people in retreat settings or special services.[3] Individuals are anointed liberally with oil. The individual says, "I anoint you with oil in the symbol of the cross, the invisible tattoo of the Lord Jesus Christ. I lay my hands on your head and pray for your wholeness." It's marvelous to see what the Holy Spirit has done in services where this particular method and words were used. However, the method isn't what accomplishes the spiritual need.

MISCONCEPTION # 4
GIFTS COME SECONDHAND
(IMPARTATION)

If you were the younger child with older siblings of the same gender, you may have a strong concept of "hand-me-downs." In an era of much larger families, this procedure definitely took place more frequently than today. A hand-me-down could be good if it was something you really liked and wanted. At last, it was now yours. On the other hand, a hand-me-down might not be so desirable if it were a piece of clothing, a toy, or even a vehicle that just "didn't do much for you."

God doesn't do hand-me-downs! He doesn't give to us what someone used and nearly wore out. He doesn't provide us with abilities having a shortened life. He doesn't offer us something just because it has been in our physical or spiritual family. He doesn't need other believers as conduits for conveying spiritual giftedness.

God doesn't need an intermediary to accomplish the placement of a spiritual gift in one's life. Since spiritual gifts are not passed genetically, there is no reason to believe your spiritual giftedness will be similar or exactly like that of your father or mother, if they were believers. Also, since spiritual giftedness is not transferred by a spiritual succession from mentors or impacting ministers, we should not assume we will be gifted in the same manner as evidenced in their lives.

As previously noted, our spiritual giftedness is by divine choice and divine impartation. No human intervention is involved in its transmission!

Yes, other believers assist us in recognizing and in operating (development for service) within our gift(s). But, no, other believers, regardless of how spiritual they may be, do not choose our gifts or transmit their giftedness.

It's amazing how in some of the more recent decades there is this move to assume the divine prerogative. A young man wrote about his most meaningful spiritual highlight by describing how a choir director passed his anointing to him. One must sincerely question concepts such as this. If the Messiah himself was anointed by the Spirit, how can we succeed with anything less?

Repeatedly the examples of Elijah-Elisha and Paul-Timothy are cited as proofs for one individual's imparting a gift to another. Each of these examples deserves close attention.

Consider the context of Elijah's situation. After the great miracle on Mount Carmel, the prophet fled in fear of Jezebel's ultimatum (1 Kings 19:1-3). Some days later in Horeb he experienced the presence of God and was given four directives. First, he was to return from where he came and he was to anoint three individuals. Two would be elevated to the position of king and one, Elisha, would be his successor. In each case, the anointing was symbolic of a new position (vv. 15-17).

Elijah's mantle was used as a symbol of the

prophetic position that would be Elisha's. Elijah threw his cloak/mantle around Elisha when he first found him (v. 19). Later, when Elijah was taken up to heaven, the mantle was allowed to fall to earth. It then became the visible symbol of Elisha's new position and authority. Elisha used it in his first miracle, which was a duplication of Elijah's last miracle (2 Kings 2:8, 13-14).

Note that Elijah didn't take the initiative in what occurred. He didn't do anything other than follow God's directives. There was no transfer of power or giftedness, only that of positional authority and responsibility.

The same appears to be true in the relationship between Paul and Timothy. There are two passages that need consideration—1 Timothy 4:14 and 2 Timothy 1:6. In these passages, Timothy was reminded of his ordination to ministry within the body of believers. The laying on of hands was a symbolic, outward action or sign of what was already inwardly placed or determined by the Holy Spirit (Num. 8:10; 27:18). Paul and the elders were simply conferring on Timothy their recognition and acceptance of God's direction.

The second reference reminded Timothy of what previously had taken place. At this point he appeared somewhat despondent at Paul's imprisonment and the heavy task at hand in

Ephesus. Paul encouraged his son in the Lord to keep the flame of faith and ministry alive. One aspect of this was being reminded of the past commitments and recognitions.

Not to be overlooked are the apostle Paul's introductory words in his letter to the Roman believers. He longed to visit with them. Unable to do so, he continually prayed for them. Paul desired to visit for the purpose of being the means for further establishing or confirming them in the faith (Rom. 1:11-12). Specifically stated are the words ". . . that I may impart to you some spiritual gift to make you strong" (NIV). Immediately following is a brief explanation of their being mutually encouraged.

Since a spiritual gift comes from and is bestowed on a person by the Holy Spirit alone, this statement cannot be referring to those things specifically listed as spiritual gifts. By necessity it must refer to a broader concept of encouraging them in the faith by both his words and example!

The bottom line continues to be that we receive our gifts from God firsthand. No human imparts gifts to us no matter how spiritual or used of God the individual may be. There are no hand-me-downs or transfers in true spirituality. It comes directly as we, by faith, submit and open ourselves to His will and work!

MISCONCEPTION # 5
GIFTS ARE HANDY SPIRITUAL TOOLS
KEPT IN STORAGE

A quote from Reinhard Bonnke needs to be the lead statement here: "He does not give it [gifts] to us to keep handy in case we can use it sometime somewhere."[4]

It's amazing how many items are kept stored in garages, closets, cupboards, and attics with the thought of possibly needing them in the future. Individuals who are children of the Depression years are especially prone to seemingly keeping everything. If you are a "boomer" kid and moved your parent's household goods, you are well aware of the phenomenon. Not to be overlooked are those individuals of all ages who fall under the label of "pack rat." That's why they have garages filled with "stuff" while vehicles are parked in the driveway. It's also why there is an ever-increasing number of storage facilities being built and rented.

Unlike "stuff," spiritual gifts are not to be considered as handy spiritual tools which may need to be utilized at some unknown time. They are to be considered as "on line" and in current operation. No, we do not control the "on" switch, but we do factor in being submissive and sensitive to what the Holy Spirit is directing.

When an individual receives a spiritual gift, it is for current operation and edification of the body of Christ. Never should we see a gift as a dormant spiritual possibility. Tied closely to this are the situations where persons are used regularly in a gift over a period of time, but then there appears to be a drought in its operation. Why is this happening? It would seem these persons will need to take a close introspection of their life. There may not be defined sin occurring, but spiritual giftedness is being put in some form of storage.

MISCONCEPTION # 6
GIFTS COME AS THE RESULT OF
INCREASED BIBLICAL KNOWLEDGE

More than likely, this is the misconception least frequently found within the Church. But, it does deserve a passing consideration. This arises from assuming that the greater one's biblical knowledge, the greater possibility for spiritual gifts to become evident in the believer's life. An element of truth may be associated here. Biblical knowledge will assist in recognizing a spiritual gift; however, it does not become the stimulus for its appearance. An individual could be able to quote every verse of the Bible, as well as share all the related material, and still have no spiritual gift evident.

No believers, regardless of how spiritual or knowledgeable, can assume this to be the stimulus for giftedness. Once again we must be reminded of their source. Spiritual gifts are the divine prerogative given by God's choice and at His timing.

MISCONCEPTION # 7
GIFTS LIE DORMANT IN THE UNBELIEVER UNTIL THE PERSON BECOMES A BELIEVER

Each time another misconception is encountered, it does cause you to wonder or speculate. How in the world did someone ever come up with such an aberrant, unsustainable idea with no biblical basis that could lend it even the slightest credibility? More than likely, such misconceptions stem from the source "I think."

The above listed misconception suggests the implanting of a spiritual gift at the point of one's birth. It remains dormant until becoming a believer and living a biblical lifestyle. This view assumes God's placing a holy gift within an unclean or sinful human. It completely disregards God's separation of sinfulness and righteousness. Also, overlooked is God's pattern of providing spiritual gifts at the appropriate time for ministry and edification to occur.

This misconception tends to remind us of the heretical belief held by some people that believers can be demon-possessed. It falls in the same error of thought.

MISCONCEPTION # 8
GIFTS ARE LIMITED TO THOSE LISTED IN SCRIPTURE

In countering this misconception great care needs to be taken not to fall prey to other errors. It's amazing how in the course of Christian history individuals have set out to correct a doctrinal or practical error only to go so far in the opposite direction to create another fallacy. This pendulum effect can be seen in the earliest centuries of the Church and forward to the present. With this in mind we approach misconception number 8 with great care.

As initially seen in chapter 1, the earliest interest in gifts focuses on the nine listed in 1 Corinthians 12:8-10. Consideration of 1 Corinthians 12:28-30, Ephesians 4:11, and Romans 12:6-8 indicates there are others as well. The issue at hand then rests on whether or not there are spiritual gifts given beyond those listed.

There is good reason to argue for there being no spiritual gifts other than those listed. First, the Scriptures include a wide variety of gifts which effectively cover the breadth of church ministry. No others are needed for as long as the Church exists. Second, a distinct listing helps to erase doubt or speculation as to whether or not a particular ability is a spiritual gift. Coupled with the realization of natural abilities provides a solid base for affirming a definite spiritual giftedness.

On the other side, we note the rather limited Scripture information provided on giftedness. As a result, there is the concept of not attempting to limit God when He hasn't limited Himself. The possibility of other gifts would seem to be a necessary position in view of distinct events. Consider the pastor who desires to minister to some of his shut-in members. He asks the Lord for the ability to play the piano. Several weeks later, he is able to play in two keys. This gift remains for the rest of his life. Then there is the minister who is in a foreign country without a translator. He begins to speak and is still able to speak fluent Spanish. He has no knowledge of the grammar and can't really tell you why he uses particular words.[5]

It would be easy to simply pass off these instances as miracles. However, they do not meet the definition or description of a miracle, which is altering the ordinary course of nature. They are truly giftings for the edification and ministry of the Church.

Accepting the possibility of there being other spiritual gifts which may be divinely conferred places a tremendous responsibility on us. Simply because someone is highly skilled in an area doesn't mean it is spiritual giftedness. Otherwise, we may fall into the heresy of believing there to be a gift of landscaping, a gift of cooking, or a gift of decorating.

MISCONCEPTION # 9
GIFTS ARE LIMITED TO INDIVIDUALS WHO HAVE EXPERIENCED PENTECOSTAL SPIRIT BAPTISM

Yes, individuals who have experienced the distinct event of Spirit baptism should more naturally be open to the operation of spiritual gifts. The fullness of the Spirit logically will be evident through these demonstrations!

Yet, we must be reminded of what the Bible states. Spiritual gifts are associated with the activity of the Holy Spirit. First Corinthians 12:11 indicates these to be the work of the Spirit in a believer's life. Nowhere in this chapter is there any discussion or reference to the event of Spirit baptism.

We become believers through the regenerating work of the Holy Spirit. From that point, the Spirit begins His presence within. This opens the door for spiritual gifts to become evident and operable.

ENDNOTES

[1] Matthew 20:20-23.

[2] Reinhard Bonnke, *Mighty Manifestations* (Orlando: Creation House, 1994) 71.

[3] Dr. Robert Webber edited the *Complete Library of Christian Worship* as well as authored a number of books such as *Worship Is a Verb*.

[4] Bonnke, *Mighty Manifestations*, 65.

[5] The individuals referred to are the late Reverend Jesse L. Wiggins and Dr. Mark Rutland respectively.

STUDY GUIDE
Chapter 12

Hopefully, no believer will shy away from spiritual gifts because of the many pitfall misconceptions. That would be like refusing to ride in a car or truck or fly in an airplane because of the possibility of accidents. Knowing the potential misconceptions enables us to avoid them while opening ourselves to be used through the ministry of spiritual gifts.

Misconception can easily creep into our thinking without realizing how and why it is taking place. Sadly, these misconceptions do not die easily once they become entrenched in our minds. In the process of our adhering to them, we can become immersed in both doctrinal and practical errors.

QUESTIONS

1. List the four reasons for misconceptions coming into existence.

2. Why are spiritual gifts not a sign of spiritual maturity?

3. What may be some aspects of the price to pay in the operation of one's giftedness?

4. What is the argument against impartation?

5. Why should spiritual gifts not be seen as tools stored for some point of need?

6. What is the main reason for knowing spiritual gifts do not come from biblical knowledge?

7. List several reasons for believing the only spiritual gifts in existence are listed in Scripture.

8. Why are spiritual gifts not limited to those who have experienced the Pentecostal expression of Spirit baptism?

13

Ministering in Your Giftedness

INTERACTIVE MEMBERS OF ONE BODY

God is not calling you to be a *spiritual superstar* but *Christ's servant to the Body*. The body of Christ is a dynamic organism. It is alive, energetic, vigorous, and functional. It is not static, idle, or inert. The body of Christ is enlivened by the power of the Holy Spirit. It is brought into being by the Almighty God, and it is sustained by divine initiative and divine power.

If the body of Christ is to be what God intended it to be, then we must operate with full understanding and full cooperation with God's direction and in God's provision. God intends the Church, the body of Christ, the people of God, to be that dynamic organism in which His

Spirit is operating. In a day of superstars and heroes, God is calling upon the people of God to align themselves, not with the model of the world, but with the divine plan and with the divine purpose. In God's plan and purpose, we are reminded that we are not called upon to outshine or outdo each other, but to find our individual places and our gifts and to allow the energizing Spirit of God to activate them in the body of Christ.

Consider the words *interactive, relational, interdependence, diversity,* and *unity*. These words are descriptive of the body of Christ. The Body is one unit with many members. The Holy Spirit incorporated us into the one Body, regardless of nationality, social status, or anything else. God created diversity in unity. Different functioning members are necessary to have a body. Every member is vital for there to be a body.

God is the Author of diversity, but not division. No member can claim to be more of the Body than another member. No member should claim to be less a part of the Body because of differences of function. God has set each member in the Body as He wished (1 Cor. 12:18). Each member should accept the place of God's choosing rather than despising it. Each member should affirm the place of every other member. God blended together the Body so that there would be no division, but that there would be the same care for each other (vv. 24-25). Mutual concern is necessary in the Body. The wholeness of the Body is dependent on the functioning of each member in right relationship. No believer can rightly say, "I do not belong to the Body." No believer can rightly say, "I do not need you."

In Romans 12, 1 Corinthians 12, and Ephesians 4, spiritual gifts are discussed in the context of the Body. Each gift is a manifestation of the Holy Spirit for the good of all (1 Cor. 12:7). The Holy Spirit apportions the gifts to each member as He purposes. The mutual interdependence and interaction are realized as the members employ the gifts for the common good. "Since spiritual gifts are relational and interactive, they serve to structure the church as a community and show forth signs of grace to the world."[1]

We are called to be Christ's servants to His body, fulfilling our place, exercising our giftedness, in order to contribute to mutual edification. "Paul would urge us to meet in dependency on one another as the vehicles of God's grace and to view the well-being and strengthening of the whole church as the primary aim of the gathering."[2] Paul's summary statement in 1 Corinthians 14:26 is "Let all things be done for edification"[3] (NKJV). Peter's exhortation agreed: "Like good stewards of the manifold grace of

God, serve one another with whatever gift each of you has received" (1 Pet. 4:10).

IMPERATIVE OF LOVE

The gifts of the Spirit are meaningless without the fruit of the Spirit. The fruit of the Spirit is a production of Christian character—Christlikeness. At the head of the fruit of the Spirit is love.

With each discussion of the spiritual gifts, love is stated as a necessity in the operation of the gifts. Following the listing of gifts in Romans 12:6-8, Paul enjoined the believers, "Let love be genuine" (v. 9) and "Love one another with mutual affection" (v. 10).

The exhortation preceding the discussion of the gifts of Christ to His church is "Forbearing one another in love" (Eph. 4:2 KJV). Christ's gifts to His church will result in growth that will enable believers to speak the truth in love (v. 15) and the Body to build itself up in love (v. 16). Believers have an intricate and intimate relationship with one another in the body of Christ. That relationship is characterized by love. Love guides believers in patient endurance as we progress together. Love brings honesty and truth-speaking. The spiritual body continues to build itself up in love.

The "love" chapter (1 Cor. 13) is strategically placed in the middle of a discussion concerning the operation of spiritual gifts (chs. 12-14). It is not merely a sentimental excursus to be recited at weddings, but a straightforward, insightful, probing, and incisive exposition of love. Paul's transition from spiritual gifts to love was "And I will show you a still more excellent way" (12:31b). Love is not a tool, not a strategy, not just a good approach—it is the most excellent *way of life*.

> Paul's point is that the love he is about to discuss cannot be classed with the *charismata*: it is not one *charisma* of many, but an entire "way" of life, an overarching, all-embracing style of life that utterly transcends in importance the claims of this or that *charisma*. Love, then, is not a *charisma* but an entire way of life without which, as we shall see, all *charismata* must be judged utterly worthless.[4]

Paul used the first person *I* in 1 Corinthians 13:1-3 probably to show that this love way of life is applicable to every believer and that the shocking statements concerning love were related to him as well. If my oratorical abilities were the best that earth and heaven could provide, if I have not love, I have become abrasive, disruptive, disturbing, and discordant. If I am highly gifted with prophetic utterances and the word of knowledge without human limitations, and I have the gift of faith which could move mountains, but I have not love, I am nothing. If

I sacrificed all my possessions and even delivered my body to become a martyr to be burned, but if I do not have love, I gain nothing.[5] From these verses we can see that giftedness or personal sacrifice without love brings dissonance, personal nothingness, and no profit.

Paul gives a description of love in 1 Corinthians 13:4-7. Let us consider some of those descriptions.

> Love wins over a short temper because it is patient, longsuffering, and endures under trial.

> Love wins over being overbearing because it is kind.

> Love wins over jealousy and envy because it trusts and serves.

> Love wins over arrogance because it is not inwardly puffed up.

> Love wins over rudeness because it practices decorum.

> Love wins over self-seeking and stubbornness because it does not seek its own way.

> Love wins over irritability because it is not provoked or exasperated.

> Love wins over resentment because it does not keep a record of evil.

> Love does not rejoice over wrong but rejoices with the truth.

> Love bears up under the heavy load and per-
> severes.
>
> Love keeps believing and keeps hoping.[6]

The Holy Spirit guided Paul to help believers to understand that love is not just some ab-
stract term. It is very practical. Love is reflected
in how we relate to God, to one another, and to
ourselves.

> Love as it is defined here, is a revelation of the
> character of God. It is, therefore, a revelation
> of God's will for humankind. Every person
> who does not love is in moral default and is
> under Divine judgment. We have not fulfilled
> God's will for us until love has become in us
> what it is in God—a personal attribute, an es-
> sential of our nature as men and women in the
> image of God.[7]

Paul concluded the chapter on love by stating unequivocally, "Love never ends" (v. 8). The
gifts of the Spirit are provided by God for His
church until He returns, and after that they will
no longer be needed. Love, on the other hand,
endures throughout eternity.

Paul connected love with spiritual gifts again
by saying, "Pursue love and strive for the spiritual gifts, and especially that you may prophesy" (14:1). Both imperative verbs are strong
words. The first one is the root word for *perse-
cute*, so "pursue" or "aim for" is appropriate.

"Keep on pursuing" is the thought. The second word is the root word for *zealous,* so "eagerly desiring" or "striving" is appropriate. Pursuing love and striving for spiritual gifts are simultaneously done. Love guides the striving for spiritual gifts, however. The reason Paul said "especially that you may prophesy" is because prophecy edifies the Body rather than edifying the individual alone. Love guides the believers to seek the gifts needed by the congregation at a given time. Love looks beyond itself to the needs of others. Love aims for the building up of the Body (vv. 3-5, 12, 26). In the operation of spiritual gifts and in the whole of the Christian life, love is the imperative.

INVESTING YOURSELF

It is the will of God for you to minister in the area of giftedness to which God has assigned you. Your involvement will bless the spiritual community, and you will be blessed in the process. No one else can fill your place. So the challenge is to find the place and fill it.

Consecrate.

Employ the spiritual disciplines of prayer, fasting, and meditating upon God's Word. Deliberately set aside some time each day to be alone with the Lord. If your body is healthy and you can fast a meal, during the time you ordinarily would give attention to eating, give special attention to God.

Cultivate sensitivity to the Holy Spirit.

Become personally familiar with the Holy Spirit's leading. Listen to Him. He will comfort, direct, teach, and guide you.

Pursue love.

Allow love to be the underlying, overarching, and permeating motive of your life. Let the desire to please God and benefit the spiritual community be your chief motivation. This pursuit will help you to be more open to what God wants and to what the Church needs rather than to your own ambitions and preferences.

Continue to grow in your knowledge concerning spiritual gifts.

Become convinced of the urgent need of the gifts of the Holy Spirit. Become convinced of the availability of the gifts of the Holy Spirit.

Develop an appreciation for the spiritual community.

Realize that you are important to the community of believers. Your fellow believers are important to you also. Affirm mutual interdependence in which each is receiving and giving. The spiritual community can help you discover the area of giftedness to which God has appointed you. Pray that God will help the spiritual community to be Christlike, and be patient while God brings that request to pass.

Assess what God has done and is seeking to do in your life.

What are some ways God has used you in the past? What opportunities of ministry have you had? What ministry involvement has offered help to others? When you get close to the Lord, what are your intense desires? Helping? Serving? Leading? Encouraging? Rescuing? Giving? Speaking? Is there a specific area of interest or burden now? Share your thoughts with the spiritual community (maybe in a small group setting) and get feedback from them. This process can bring confirmation concerning God's will.

Trust God to reveal His plan and direct your steps.

The all-wise God knows you perfectly, and He knows the needs of His church. He does not want you to be continually frustrated in trying to find His will. He delights in informing you of His plans for your life and of your place in His work. What an awesome opportunity! Use your natural abilities for the glory of God and believe

God to provide supernatural abilities at the appropriate times.

Submit to the prompting of the Holy Spirit.

Do not allow timidity or fear to hinder your cooperating with the Holy Spirit. Do not demand that God lead you in a certain way. Be thankful that God provides everything the spiritual community needs—and that the gifts He assigns to you are part of that provision.

ENDNOTES

[1] Frank D. Macchia, *Baptized in the Spirit* (Grand Rapids: Zondervan, 2006) 242.

[2] David Peterson, *Engaging with God* (Downers Grove, IL: IVP Academics, 1992) 214.

[3] Note Paul's use of "edification" in 1 Corinthians 14:3-5, 12, 17, and 26.

[4] D. A. Carson, *Showing the Spirit* (Grand Rapids: Baker Books, 1987) 56-57.

[5] Author's expanded paraphrase of 1 Corinthians 13:1-3.

[6] Author's expanded paraphrase of 1 Corinthians 12:4-7.

[7] R. Hollis Gause, *Living in the Spirit: The Way of Salvation* (Cleveland, TN: Self-published, 2006) 280.

STUDY GUIDE
Chapter 13

Christ is the Head and we are the members of His body. As we fulfill our individual places relationally and interactively in the Body, we together bring glory to God. We also grow to maturity and testify to unbelievers of the reality of transformation in Christ. The imperative of love is expressed by Jesus Christ, "By this everyone will know that you are my disciples, if you have love for one another" (John 12:35).

QUESTIONS

1. Review the emphasis on the Body in each of the scriptural locations concerning spiritual gifts.

2. How do the words *interdependence, relational,* and *interactive* characterize the spiritual body?

3. How is love made prominent in the discussions concerning spiritual gifts?

4. On what basis can it be said that love is imperative in relationship to spiritual gifts?

5. Formulate a personal plan to pursue love and to strive for spiritual gifts.

Other Pathway titles by these authors:

Dr. John A. Lombard Jr.
Speaking for God

Dr. Jerald J. Daffe
In the Face of Evil

Life Challenges for Men

Revival: God's Plan for His People

*A Minister's Service Manual
for Contemporary Church Celebrations*

Dr. John A. Lombard Jr.
and
Dr. Jerald J. Daffe

*Speaking in Tongues: Initial
Evidence of Spirit Baptism?*